McFool's©
Best Internet Humor

Year 2000 Edition

Written by Thousands

Compiled by Alister McFool

"The people's humor – outrageously funny"

McFool's©
Best Internet Humor

Year 2000 Edition

Written by Thousands

All rights reserved.
No part of this book may be used or reproduced in any manner whatsoever without written permission of the publuisher.

Printed in the United States of America.
ISBN: 1-891231-23-5
Library of Congress Catalog Card Number: 00-132174

Word Association Publishers
205 Fifth Avenue
Tarentum, Pennsylvania 15084

Dedication

Where do jokes come from? A man I know, an eccentric millionaire, was obsessed with finding the real source of good humor. He started back tracking new jokes, going from one person to the next asking each the same question, "Who did you hear that joke from?"

His journey took him all around the world, and as time went on he found himself more and more at what he felt was ground zero, the source point, the promised land. It was a non-descript bar on New York's West Side.

After much needling, the bartender revealed that a man came in about once a month and told the patrons one great never-been-heard joke after another. The eccentric millionaire waited patiently night after night for this man to reveal himself. Sure enough, this man came in, a group of eager people would gather around, and he told 15 to 20 great jokes and then left.

The millionaire's obsession only grew, and he followed the man to a cheap hotel. The man ignored him and the millionare began to camp out in the dim dank hallway hoping to learn more. Finally, the man called him in to his funky room, sat him down, and pulled off his mask to reveal an alien being with one eye. The alien said, "You're race has a high probability of blowing up the world, I have been sent to save you, and the only thing that lightens you people up is humor." "So, I am forced to use my genius to think up jokes to lighten the tension. Now, get out."

Many of these jokes originated from that alien, and I would like to dedicate this book to him for his selfless service. Never underestimate the improtance of humor!

Bear Hunting (G)
Two men went bear hunting. While one stayed in the cabin, the other went out looking for a bear. He soon found a huge bear, shot at it but only wounded it. The enraged bear charged toward him, he dropped his rifle and started running for the cabin as fast as he could. He ran pretty fast but the bear was just a little faster and gained on him with every step. Just as he reached the open cabin door, he tripped and fell flat. Too close behind to stop, the bear tripped over him and went rolling into the cabin. The man jumped up, closed the cabin door and yelled to his friend inside, "You skin this one while I go and get another!"

Elevator Ride (PG-13)
A blonde & brunette are in an elevator. On the third floor a man gets in who looks perfect -- 3-piece suit, great build, nice butt. The bad part is they both noticed he had dandruff. The man got off on the 5th floor. Once the doors closed, the brunette turned to the blonde and said, "Someone should give him Head & Shoulders. "To which the blonde replied, "How do you give shoulders?"

The Insured Cigars (G)
A North Carolina man, having bought several expensive cigars, insured them against... get this... fire. After he had smoked them, he then decided that he had a claim against the insurance company and filed. The insurance company refused to pay, citing the obvious reason that the man had consumed the cigar normally. The man sued. The judge stated that since the company had insured the cigars against fire, they were

obligated to pay. After the man accepted payment for his claim, the company then had him arrested ..... for arson.

Virgin Couple On Their Wedding Night (R)

A young virgin couple are finally wed. Each one is nervous about the impending night, but neither are willing to admit or ask each other about it. Wondering what to do first, the young man calls his father.

"Pop, what do I do first?"

"Get naked and climb into bed," his father replies.

So, the young man does as he is advised. The girl is mortified and calls her mama.

"Get naked and join him," is the advice from mama, so she complies.

After laying there for a few moments, the young man excuses himself and calls his dad again.

"What do I do?" he asks.

His father replies, "Look at her naked body. Then, take the hardest part of your body and put it where she pees!" is the dad's advice.

A few moments later, the girl again calls her mama. "What do I do now?" she asks.

"Well, what is he doing?" mama asks.

"He's in the bathroom, dunking his head in the toilet!"

Believe it or not (G)
SKELETON

A 63yr old widow was admitted to the hospital in Recife, Brazil, suffering abdominal pains. X-rays showed that she was carrying a 20 inch long skeleton of a fetus which she conceived a decade earlier. It had become lodged outside the womb and was never expelled from her body.

Honey, Do Anything He Wants (PG-13)

An escaped convict broke into a house and tied up a young couple who had been sleeping in the bedroom. As soon as he had a chance, the husband turned to his voluptuous young wife, bound-up on the bed in a skimpy nightgown, and whispered, "Honey, this guy hasn't seen a woman in years. Just cooperate with anything he wants. If he wants to have sex with you, just go along with it and pretend you like it. Our lives depend on it!"

"Dear," the wife hissed, spitting out her gag, "I'm so relieved you feel that way, because he just told me he thinks you have a really nice, tight-looking ass!!!!!!!"

How you know you're in Southern California (G)

1. Your co-worker tells you she has 8 body piercings... and none are visible.
2. You make over $250,000 and still can't afford a house.
3. You take a bus and are shocked at 2 people carrying on a conversation in English.
4. Your child's 3rd grade teacher has purple hair, a nose ring and is named Breeze.
5. You can't remember... is pot illegal?
6. You've been to more than one baby shower that has two mothers and a sperm donor.
7. A low-speed police pursuit will interrupt ANY TV broadcast
8. Your best friends just named their twins after her acting coach and his personal trainer.
9. Your car insurance costs as much as your house payment
10. It's sprinkling and there's a report on every news station about "STORM WATCH '99"
11. You call 911 and they put you on hold.

OUCH AND DOUBLE OUCH! (R)
A couple hobbled into a Washington (state) emergency room covered in bloody restaurant towels. The man had his around his waist and the woman had hers around her head. They eventually explained to doctors that they had gone out that evening for a romantic dinner. Overcome with passion, the woman crept under the table to administer oral sex to the man. While in the act, she had an epileptic fit, which caused her to clamp down on the man's penis and wrench it from side to side. In agony and desperation, the man grabbed a fork and stabbed her in the head until she let go.

LETTER FROM CAMP (G)
Dear Mom,

Our scout master told us all write to our parents in case you saw the flood on TV and worried. We are OK. Only 1 of our tents and 2 sleeping bags got washed away. Luckily, none of us got drowned because we were all up on the mountain looking for Chad when it happened. Oh yes, please call Chad's mother and tell her he is OK. He can't write because of the cast.

I got to ride in one of the search & rescue jeeps. It was neat. We never would have found him in the dark if it hadn't been for the lightning. Scoutmaster Webb got mad at Chad for going on a hike alone without telling anyone. Chad said he did tell him, but it was during the fire so he probably didn't hear him. Did you know that if you put gas on a fire the gas can will blow up?

The wet wood still didn't burn, but one of our tents did. Also some of our clothes. John is going to look weird until his hair grows back.

Guess what? We have all passed our first aid merit badges. When Dave dove in the lake and cut his arm, we got to see how a tourniquet works. Also Wade and I threw up.

Scoutmaster Webb said it probably was just food poisoning from the leftover chicken, he said they got sick that way with the food they ate in prison. I'm so glad he got out and became our scoutmaster. He said he sure figured out how to get things done better and enjoy male company while he was doing his time.

I have to go now. We are going into town to mail our letters and buy bullets. Don't worry about anything.

>We are fine.
>Love, Tommy

WHAT WAS PLAN B??? (G)

An Illinois man, pretending to have a gun, kidnapped a motorist and forced him to drive to two different automated teller machines. The kidnapper then proceeded to withdraw money from his own bank account.

TOO ROUGH (G)

A little girl asked her mother, "Can I go outside and play with the boys?"

Her mother replied, "No, you can't play with the boys, they're too rough."

The little girl thought about it for a few moments and asked, "If I can find a smooth one, can I play with him?"

GRAVITY KILLS (Darwin Award) (G)

A 22-year-old Reston man was found dead after he tried to use Bungee straps (the stretchy little ropes with hooks on each end) to bungee jump off a 70-foot railroad trestle, police said. Fairfax County police said Eric Barcia, a fast-food worker, taped a bunch of these straps together, wrapped an end around one foot, anchored the other end to the trestle at Lake Accotink Park, jumped...and hit the pavement. Warren Carmichael, a police spokesman, said investigators think Barcia was alone because his car was found nearby. "The length of the cord that he had assembled was greater than the distance between the trestle and the ground," Carmichael said.

Declaration of Independence (G)

A Kentucky teacher was quizzing her students. "Johnny, who signed the Declaration of Independence?"

He said, "Damn if I know."

She was a little put out by his swearing, so she told him to go home and to bring his father with him when he came back. Next day, the father came with his son, sat in the back of the room to observe. She started back in on her quiz and finally got back to the boy. "Now, Johnny, I'll ask you again. Who signed the Declaration of Independence?"

"Well, hell, teacher," Johnny said, "I told you I didn't know."

The father jumped up in the back, pointed a stern finger at his son, and said,

"Johnny, if you signed that damn thing, hell, you damn well better admit it!"

The Kiss (G)

Once upon a time, a beautiful, independent, self-assured princess happened upon a frog in a pond. The frog said to the princess: "I was once a handsome prince until an evil witch put a spell on me. One kiss from you and I will turn back into a prince and then we can marry, move into the castle with my mom, and you can prepare my meals, clean my clothes, bear my children and forever feel happy doing so." That night, while the princess dined on frog's legs, she laughed to herself and thought, "I don't think so."

Questions Asked of Kids (G)

WHAT DO MOST PEOPLE DO ON A DATE?

"On the first date, they just tell each other lies, and that usually gets them interested enough to go for a second date."
Martin, age 10

"Dates are for having fun, and people should use them to get to know each other. Even boys have something to say if you listen long enough." *Lynnette, age 8*

HOW TO YOU DECIDE WHO TO MARRY?

"No person really decides before they grow up who they're going to marry. God decides it all way before, and you get to find out later who you're stuck with." *Kirsten, age 10*

WHAT IS THE RIGHT AGE TO GET MARRIED?

"Twenty-three is the best age because you know the person FOREVER by then." *Camille, age 10*

HOW CAN A STRANGER TELL IF TWO PEOPLE ARE MARRIED?
"Married people usually look happy to talk to other people."
Eddie, age 6

"You might have to guess, based on whether they seem to be yelling at the same kids." *Derrick, age 8*

WHAT DO YOU THINK YOUR MOM AND DAD HAVE IN COMMON?
"Both don't want no more kids." *Lori, age 8*

WHAT WOULD YOU DO ON A FIRST DATE THAT WAS TURNING SOUR?
"I'd run home and play dead. The next day I would call all the newspapers and make sure they wrote about me in all the dead columns."
Craig, age 9

HOW WOULD THE WORLD BE DIFFERENT IF PEOPLE DIDN'T GET MARRIED?
"There sure would be a lot of kids to explain, wouldn't there?" *Kelvin, age 8*

"You can be sure of one thing--the boys would come chasing after us just the same as they do now." *Roberta, age 7*

LAUNCHED ON THE FOURTH OF JULY (Darwin Award)

Three young men in Oklahoma were enjoying the Fourth of July holiday and wanted to apparently test fire some fireworks. Their only real problem was that their launch pad and seating arrangements were atop a several hundred thousand-gallon fuel distillation storage tank. Oddly enough, some fumes were ignited, producing a fireball seen for miles. They were launched several hundred feet into the air and were found dead 250 yards from their respective seats.

WHY DID THE CHICKEN CROSS THE ROAD? (G)
Pat Buchanan:
   To steal a job from a decent, hardworking American.

Louis Farrakhan:
   The road, you will see, represents the black man. The chicken crossed the "black man" in order to trample him and keep him down.

Colonel Sanders:
   I missed one?!

Richard M. Nixon:
   The chicken did not cross the road. I repeat, the chicken did not cross the road. I don't know any chickens. I have never known any chickens.

Ernest Hemingway:
   To die. In the rain.

Grandpa:
   In my day, we didn't ask why the chicken crossed the road. Someone told us that the chicken crossed the road, and that was good enough for us.

Fox Mulder:
   You saw it cross the road with your own eyes. How many

more chickens have to cross before you believe it?

Bill Gates:
I have just released Chicken Coop 98, which will not only cross roads, but will lay eggs, file your important documents, and balance your check book-and Explorer is an inextricable part of the operating system. Live with it!

WITH A LITTLE HELP FROM OUR FRIENDS! (G)

Police in Oakland, California spent two hours attempting to subdue a gunman who had barricaded himself inside his home. After firing ten tear gas canisters, officers discovered that the man was standing beside them, shouting out to give himself up.

Pardon Me (G)

A young woman was depressed because she was so flat-chested. So when her fairy godmother appeared one day and offered to grant her most heartfelt wish, the young woman instantly requested large breasts.

"All right, my dear," said her fairy godmother. "From this moment on, every time a man says 'Pardon' to you, your breasts will grow."

The next day the woman was walking down the sidewalk, lost in thought, when she bumped into a policeman. "Pardon me," said the cop politely.

Her breasts grew an inch. She was ecstatic.

A few days later the young woman was doing her shopping at the supermarket.

Leaving with a large bag of groceries, she bumped into a another customer.

"Pardon me," the guy said, bending over to help her collect her groceries.

The young woman's breasts grew another inch. Very happy, she decided to treat herself to dinner at a Chinese restaurant.

Going in the door, she collided with a waiter, who bowed and said, "Oh, miss, I beg of you a thousand pardons."

Headline in the paper the next day read:
CHINESE WAITER KILLED BY TWO TORPEDOES.

SOME DAYS, IT JUST DOESN'T PAY!

Fire investigators on Maui have determined the cause of a blaze that destroyed a $127,000 home last month - a short in the homeowner's newly installed fire prevention alarm system. "This is even worse than last year," said the distraught homeowner, "when someone broke in and stole my new security system..."

Engineers Vs Lawyers (G)

Three lawyers and three engineers are traveling by train to a conference. At the station, the three lawyers each buy tickets and watch as the three engineers buy only a single ticket.

"How are three people going to travel on only one ticket?" asked one of the three lawyers.

"Watch and you'll see," answers one of the engineers.
They all board the train. The lawyers take their respective seats but all three engineers cram into a restroom and close the door behind them. Shortly after the train has departed, the conductor comes around collecting tickets. He knocks on the restroom door and says, "Ticket, please." The door opens just a crack and a single arm emerges with a ticket in hand. The

conductor takes it and moves on.

The lawyers saw this and agreed it was quite a clever idea. So after the conference, the lawyers decide to copy the engineers on the return trip and save some money. When they get to the station, they buy a single ticket for the return trip. To their astonishment, the engineers don't buy a ticket at all.

"How are you going to travel without a ticket," asks one perplexed lawyer.

"Watch and you'll see," says one of the engineers.

When they board the train, the three lawyers cram into a restroom and the three engineers cram into another one nearby. The train departs. Shortly afterward, one of the engineers leaves his restroom and walks over to the restroom where the lawyers are hiding. He knocks on the door and says, "Ticket, please."

DON'T ASK GOD TO PROVE HIMSELF, HE JUST MIGHT (G) (Darwin Award)

A lawyer and two buddies were fishing on Caddo Lake in Texas when a lightning storm hit the lake. Most of the other boats immediately headed for the shore, but not our friend the lawyer. Alone on the rear of his aluminum bass boat with his buddies, this individual stood up, spread his arms wide (crucifixion style) and shouted: "HERE I AM LORD, LET ME HAVE IT!" Needless to say, God delivered. The other two passengers on the boat survived the lightning strike with minor burns.

THE GETAWAY! (G)

A man walked into a Topeka, Kansas Kwik Shop and asked for all the money in the cash drawer. Apparently, the take was too small so he tied up the store clerk and worked the counter himself for three hours until police showed up and grabbed him.

A Wife's Love (G)
A woman's husband had been slipping in and out of a coma for several months, yet she had stayed by his bedside every single day. One day, when he came to, he motioned for her to come nearer. As she sat by him, he whispered, eyes full of tears, "My dearest, you have been with me all through the bad times. When I got fired, you were there to support me. When my business failed, you were there. When I got shot, you were by my side. When we lost the house, you stayed right here. When my health started failing, you were still by my side. You know what?"

"What dear?" she gently asked, smiling as her heart began to fill with warmth.

"I think you're bad luck."

Cheap Thrill (R).
This man was in a long line at the grocery store. As he got to the register he realized he had forgotten to get condoms. So he asked the checkout girl if she could have some condoms brought up to the register.

She asked, "What size condoms?"

The customer replied that he didn't know. She asked him to drop his pants. He did, she reached over the counter, grabbed hold of him, then picked up the store intercom and said "One box of large condoms to register 5."

The next man in line thought this was interesting and, like most of us, up for a cheap thrill. When he got to the register, he told the checker that he too had forgotten to get condoms, and asked if she could have some brought up to the register. She asked him what size, and he stated that he didn't know. She asked him to drop his pants. He did, she gave him a quick feel, picked up the store intercom and said, "One box of medium sized condoms to register 5."

A few customers back was a teen-aged boy. He thought

what he had witnessed was way too cool. He never had any type of sexual contact with a female, so he thought this was his chance. When he got up to the register, he told the checker he needed some condoms. She asked him what size, and he said he didn't know. She asked him to drop his pants and he did. She reached over the counter, gave him one quick squeeze, then picked up the intercom and said, "Clean up at register 5!"

Sex Lecture (PG-13)

The dean of women at an exclusive girls' school was lecturing her students on sexual morality.

"We live today in very difficult times for young people. In moments of temptation," she said, "ask yourself just one question: Is an hour of pleasure worth a lifetime of shame?"

A young woman rose in the back of the room and said, "Excuse me, but how do you make it last an hour?"

Chemistry Final Exam (G)

Two guys were taking Chemistry at the University of Alabama. They did pretty well on all of the quizzes and the midterms and labs, such that going into the final they had a solid "A." These two friends were so confident going into the final that the weekend before finals week (even though the Chemistry final was on Monday), they decided to go up to the University of Tennessee and party with some friends. They had a great time.

However, with hangovers and everything, they overslept all day Sunday and didn't make it back to Alabama until early Monday morning. Rather than taking the final then, they found their professor after the final to explain to him why they missed the final. They told him that they went up to the University of Tennessee for the weekend, and had planned to come back in time to study, but that they had a flat tire on the way back, and didn't have a spare, and couldn't get help for a long time, so they were late in getting back to campus.

The professor thought this over and told them they could make up the final on the following day. The two guys were elated and relieved. They studied that night and went in the next day for the final.

The professor placed them in separate rooms, and handed each of them a test booklet and told them to begin. They looked at the first problem, which was worth 5 Points. It was something simple about Molarity & Solutions.

"Cool," they thought. "This is going to be easy." They did that problem and then turned the page.

They were not prepared, however, for what they saw on this page.

It said: Which tire? (95 Points)

The Gorgeous Red Head (R)

A man walks into a bar and sits next to a gorgeous redhead.

"Can I buy you a drink?" he asks.

"Sure, but it won't do you any good, I'm a lesbian." "No way" says the man, "No woman as good looking as you could be a lesbian."

To which the woman replies "Oh yeah? See that brunette sitting at the end of the bar? I'd love nothing more than to get between her legs and lick her till she can't walk.

The red head looks at the man, who now has tears streaming down his face.

"I'm sorry," she says, "did I offend you?"

"No" the man sobs, "but I think I'm a lesbian too!"

Fourteen (G)

Walking past the big wooden fence around the insane asylum, a guy hears everyone inside chanting, "Thirteen! Thirteen! Thirteen!"

His curiosity piqued, he finds a hole in the fence and looks inside.

All of a sudden a finger shoots through the hole and pokes out his eye, and the inmates start wildly chanting, "Fourteen! Fourteen! Fourteen!"

A Rhino of a Story [Darwin Award (G)]

A Vermont native, Ronald Demuth, found himself in a difficult position. While touring the Eagle's Rock African Safari (Zoo) with a group of businessmen from St. Petersburg, Russia, Mr. Demuth went overboard to show them one of America's many marvels. He demonstrated the effectiveness of "Crazy Glue"... the hard way. Apparently, Mr. Demuth wanted to demonstrate just how good the adhesive was, so he put about 3 ounces of the adhesive in the palms of his hands, and jokingly placed them on the buttocks of a passing rhino.

The rhino, a resident of the zoo for the past thirteen years, was not initially startled as it has been part of the petting exhibit since its arrival as a baby. However, once it became aware of its being involuntarily stuck to Mr. Demuth, it began to panic and ran around the petting area wildly making Mr. Demuth run behind. "Sally the rhino hasn't been feeling well lately. She had been very constipated. We had just given her a laxative and some depressants to relax her bowels, when Mr. Demuth played his juvenile prank," said James Douglass, caretaker.

During Sally's tirade two fences were destroyed, a shed wall was gored, and a number of small animals escaped. Also, during the stampede, three pygmy goats and one duck were stomped to death.

As for Demuth, it took a team of medics and zoo caretakers' to remove his hands from her buttocks. First, the animal had to be captured and calmed down. However, during this process the laxatives began to take hold and Mr. Demuth was repeatedly showered with over 30 gallons of rhino diarrhea. "It was tricky. We had to calm her down, while at the same time shield our faces from being pelted with rhino dung.

I guess you could say that Mr. Demuth was into it up to his neck. Once she was under control, we had three people with shovels working to keep an air passage open for Mr. Demuth. We were able to tranquilize her and apply a solvent to remove his hands from her rear," said Douglass. I don't think he'll be playing with Crazy Glue for awhile."

Meanwhile, the Russians, while obviously amused, also were impressed with the power of the adhesive. "I'm going to buy some for my children, but of course they can't take it to the zoo," commented Vladimir Zolnikov.

That Old Kentucky Taste (G)

A nurse caring for a woman from Kentucky asked, "So how's your breakfast this morning?" "It's very good, except for the Kentucky Jelly. I can't seem to get used to the taste," the patient replied. The nurse asked to see the jelly and the woman produced a foil packet labeled "KY Jelly."

A Man's Got to Do What a Man's Got to Do (PG-13)

Two men were adrift in a life boat following a dramatic escape from a burning freighter. While rummaging through the boat's provisions, One of the men stumbled across an old lamp. Secretly hoping that a Genie would appear, he rubbed the lamp vigorously. To the amazement of the castaways, one did come forth.

This particular Genie, however, stated that she could only deliver one wish, not the standard three. Without giving much thought to the matter the man blurted out: "Make the entire ocean into beer!"

Immediately the Genie clapped her hands with a deafening crash the entire sea turned into the finest brew ever sampled by mortals.

Simultaneously, the Genie vanished to her freedom. Only the gentle lapping of beer on the hull broke the stillness as the two men considered their circumstances.

The other man looked disgustedly at the one whose wish had been granted. After a long, tension filled moment, he spoke: "Nice going! Now we're going to have to pee in the boat."

THE REAL MEANING BEHIND THE ABBREVIATIONS IN PERSONAL ADS (PG-13)

FIRST THE WOMEN:

40-ish	48
Adventurer	Has had more partners than you ever will
Athletic	Flat Chested
Average looking	Ugly
Beautiful	Pathological liar
Contagious Smile	Bring your penicillin
Educated	College dropout
Emotionally Secure	Medicated
Feminist	Fat; ball buster
Free spirit	Substance user
Friendship first	Trying to live down reputation as ####
Fun	Annoying
Gentle	Comatose
Good Listener	Borderline Autistic
New-Age	All body hair, all the time

Old-fashioned	Lights out, missionary position only
Open-minded	Desperate
Outgoing	Loud
Passionate	Loud
Poet	Depressive Schizophrenic
Professional	Real Witch
Romantic	Looks better by candle light
Voluptuous	Very Fat
Weight proportional to height	Hugely Fat
Wants Soulmate	One step away from stalking
Widow	Nagged first husband to death
Young at heart	Toothless crone

THE MALE SIDE OF THE LIST

40-ish	52 and looking for 25-yr-old
Athletic	Sits on the couch and watches ESPN
Average looking	Unusual hair growth on ears, nose, and back
Educated	Will always treat you like an idiot
Free Spirit	Sleeps with your sister
Friendship first	As long as friendship involves nudity
Fun	Good with a remote and a six pack
Good looking	Arrogant
Honest	Pathological Liar
Huggable	Overweight, more body hair than a bear
Like to cuddle	Insecure, overly dependent
Mature	Until you get to know him
Open-minded	Wants to sleep with your sister but she's Not interested.
Physically fit	I spend a lot of time in front of mirror admiring myself
Poet	Has written on a bathroom stall
Spiritual	Once went to church with his grand mother on Easter Sunday
Stable	Occasional stalker, but never arrested
Thoughtful	Says 'Please' when demanding a beer

Darwin Award Runner-Up (G)

RENTON, WA, USA. A Renton, Washington man tried to commit a robbery. This was probably his first attempt, as suggested by the fact that he had no previous record of violent crime, and by his terminally stupid choices as listed below:
1. The target was H&J Leather & Firearms...a gun shop.
2. The shop was full of customers, in a state where a substantial portion of the adult population is licensed to carry concealed handguns in public places.
3. To enter the shop, he had to step around a marked Police patrol car parked at the front door.
4. An officer in uniform was standing next to the counter, having coffee before reporting to duty. Upon seeing the officer, the would-be robber announced a holdup and fired a few wild shots. The officer and a clerk promptly returned fire, removing him from the gene pool. Several other customers also drew their guns, but didn't fire. No one else was hurt.

Bet in a Bar (PG-13)

Guy in a bar says to the bartender, "I'll bet you $300 that I can piss directly into a glass on the other side of the bar, over 20 feet away, without spilling a drop of piss anywhere" Bartender says, "Sure, I'll take that bet"

Guy proceeds to unzip his pants and starts pissing EVERYWHERE! On the floor, on the bar counter, on himself, on the bartender, piss is just flying everywhere EXCEPT in the glass! Bartender laughs while all of this is going on, thinking he is going to be $300 richer in a minute. Guy pulls out $300 and hands it over to the bartender smiling while he does it. The bartender says, "Hey, you just lost $300, what are you so happy about?" Guy says, "Well you see that bunch of guys back there playing pool? I just bet each one of them $500 that I could come over here and piss on your bar, piss on your floor and piss on you and not only would you not be angry, you'd be happy about it!"

DO-IT-YOURSELF BRAIN SURGERY?? (G)

In Ohio, an unidentified man in his late twenties walked into a police station with a 9-inch wire protruding from his forehead and calmly asked officers to give him an X-ray to help him find his brain, which he claimed had been stolen. Police were shocked to learn that the man had drilled a 6-inch deep hole in his skull with a Black & Decker power drill and had stuck the wire in to try and find the missing brain

Sex with the Teacher (R)

A 13 year-old boy comes home from school and his Mom asks how his day was. He replies, "I had sex with my teacher today."

"Oh my God! You get to your room! Wait till your father comes home!!!", says the Mom.

A while later the father comes home and the Mom says, "Go up to your son's room and talk to him. He's been really bad today."

Dad goes up to the son's room and asks why Mom is so mad. "I told her I had sex with my teacher today, replied the boy.

"All right! That's my boy!" says dad. "Ya know son, women just don't think like men. But I'm proud of you. What are you now, about thirteen, right? Wow. That's my son! Ya know what? I'm so proud of you I'm gonna take you out and buy you that new shiny bike you've been wanting!"

So the dad and his son go out and buy the nicest, reddest, shiniest bike in the whole town. "You gonna ride it home son?"

asks dad.

The boy replied, "Nah, my butt is still sore."

Moving Story (G)

It all began in 1862 during the Civil War, when Union Army Captain Robert Ellicombe was with his men near Harrison's Landingin Virginia. The Confederate Army was on the other side of the narrow strip of land.

During the night, Captain Ellicombe heard the moan of a soldier who lay mortally wounded on the field. Not knowing if it was a Union or Confederate soldier, the captain decided to risk his life and bring the stricken man back for medical attention.

Crawling on his stomach through the gunfire, the captain reached the stricken soldier and began pulling him toward his encampment. When the captain finally reached his own lines, he discovered it was actually a Confederate soldier, but the soldier was dead. The captain lit a lantern. Suddenly, he caught his breath and went numb with shock. In the dim light, he saw the face of the soldier. It was his own son. The boy had been studying music in the South when the war broke out. Without telling his father, he enlisted in the Confederate Army.

The following morning, heartbroken, the father asked permission of his superiors to give his son a full military burial despite his enemy status. His request was partially granted. The captain had asked if he could have a group of Army band members play a funeral dirge for the son at the funeral. That request was turned down since the soldier was a Confederate. Out of respect for the father, they did say they could give him only one musician.

The captain chose a bugler. He asked the bugler to play a series of musical notes he had found on a piece of paper in the pocket of his dead son's uniform. This wish was granted. This music was the haunting melody we now know as "Taps" that is used at all military funerals.

These are the words to "TAPS":
Day is done,
Gone the sun,
From the lakes,
From the hills,
From the sky.
All is well.
Safely rest.
God is nigh.

DARWIN AWARD WINNER FOR 1997 ANNOUNCED (G)

The Darwin Awards-An annual honor given to the person who did the gene pool the biggest service by killing themselves in the most extraordinarily stupid way. The 1995 winner was the fellow who was killed by a Coke machine which toppled over on top of him as he was attempting to tip a free soda out of it.

And now, the 1997 winner: Larry Waters of Los Angeles- one of the few Darwin winners to survive his award-winning accomplishment. Larry's boyhood dream was to fly. When he graduated from high school, he joined the Air Force in hopes of becoming a pilot. Unfortunately, poor eyesight disqualified him. When he was finally discharged, he had to satisfy himself with watching jets fly over his backyard.

One day, Larry had a bright idea. He decided to fly. He went to the local Army-Navy surplus store and purchased 45 weather balloons and several tanks of helium. The weather balloons, when fully inflated, would measure more than four feet across. Back home, Larry securely strapped the balloons to his sturdy lawn chair. He anchored the chair to the bumper of his jeep and inflated the balloons with the helium. He climbed on for a test while it was still only a few feet above the ground.

Satisfied it would work, Larry packed several sandwiches and a six-pack of Miller Lite, loaded his pellet gun-figuring he could pop a few balloons when it was time to descend, and went back to the floating lawn chair. He tied himself in along with his pellet gun and provisions. Larry's plan was to lazily float up to a height of about 30 feet above his back yard after severing the anchor and in a few hours come back down.

Things didn't quite work out that way. When he cut the cord anchoring the lawn chair to his jeep, he didn't float lazily up to 30 or so feet. Instead he streaked into the LA sky as if shot from a cannon. He didn't level off at 30 feet, nor 100 feet. After climbing and climbing, he leveled off at 11,000 feet. At that height he couldn't risk shooting any of the balloons, lest he unbalance the load and really find himself in trouble. So he stayed there, drifting, cold and frightened, for more than 14 hours.

Then he really got in trouble. He found himself drifting into the primary approach corridor of the Los Angeles International Airport. A United pilot first spotted Larry. He radioed the tower and described passing a guy in a lawn chair with a gun. Radar confirmed the existence of an object floating 11,000 feet above the airport.

LAX emergency procedures swung into full alert and a helicopter was dispatched to investigate. LAX is right on the ocean. Night was falling and the offshore breeze began to flow. It carried Larry out to sea with the helicopter in hot pursuit. Several miles out, the helicopter caught up with Larry, Once the crew determined that Larry was not dangerous, they attempted to close in for a rescue but the draft from the blades would push Larry away whenever they neared.

Finally, the helicopter ascended to a position several hundred feet above Larry and lowered a rescue line. Larry snagged the line and was hauled back to shore. The difficult maneuver was flawlessly executed by the helicopter crew.

As soon as Larry was hauled to earth, he was arrested by waiting members of the LAPD for violating LAX airspace. As he was led away in handcuffs, a reporter dispatched to cover the daring rescue asked why he had done it. Larry stopped, turned and replied nonchalantly, "A man can't just sit around." Lets hear it for Larry Waters, the 1997 Darwin Award Winner.

Prim and Proper (R)

A rather prim and proper woman is riding the Greyhound bus from Shreveport to New Orleans. It's been a long day and she"s bored. She knows it's not right but she decides to listen to the two Cajun men sitting behind her.

Cajun #1: "Naw, naw, naw! How many time I gotta tell ya! First, Emma cums... din I cums... din da 2 asses, dey cums... din I cums agin..."

Cajun #2: "That's ain't how I learnt it!"

Well, Miss Prim & Proper is thinking, "Oh, my Lord!". She tries to tune them out, but is unsuccessful.

Cajun #1: "Igit, shad-up and lemme splain! First, Emma cums...din I cums...din da 2 asses, dey cums...din I cums agin...din da 2 asses, dey cums agin..."

Cajun #2: "And din what?"

Cajun #1: "Din I cums agin..."

Well, Miss Prim & Proper just can't take it anymore. She turns around in her seat to set the Cajuns straight.

Lady: "Sirs, obviously your parents failed to teach you that it is highly improper to discuss such matters in public! I must insist that you cease this foul discussion immediately!"

Cajun #2: "Lady, we ain't tawkin 'bout no birds."

Lady: "That is disgusting and most inappropriate!!!"

Cajun #2: "Alright, Lady, how do YOU spell Mississippi?"

1999 DARWIN AWARD WINNER IS (G)....

MANITOBA, CANADA. Telephone relay company night watchman Edward Baker, 31, was killed early Christmas morning by excessive microwave radiation exposure. He was apparently attempting to keep warm next to a telecommunications feed-horn.

Baker had been suspended on a safety violation once last year, according to Northern Manitoba Signal Relay spokesperson Anya Cooke.

She noted that Baker's earlier infraction was for defeating a safety shut-off switch and entering a restricted maintenance catwalk in order to stand in front of the microwave dish. He had told coworkers that it was the only way he could stay warm during his twelve-hour shift at the station, where winter temperatures often dip to forty below zero .Microwaves can heat water molecules within human tissue in the same way that they heat food in microwave ovens.

For his Christmas shift, Baker reportedly brought a twelve pack of beer and a plastic lawn chair, which he positioned directly in line with the strongest microwave beam. Baker had not been told about a tenfold boost in microwave power planned that night to handle the anticipated increase in holiday long-distance calling traffic. Baker's body was discovered by the daytime watchman, John Burns, who was greeted by an odor he mistook for a Christmas roast he thought Baker must have prepared as a surprise. Burns also reported to NMSR company officials that Baker's unfinished beers had exploded.

ARE WE COMMUNICATING?? (G)

A man spoke frantically into the phone, "My wife is pregnant and her contractions are only two minutes apart!" "Is this her first child?" the doctor asked. "No, you idiot!" the man shouted, "this is her husband!"

Mary's Diary (PG-13)

After dinner and a movie, Carl drove his date to a quiet country road and made his move. When Mary responded enthusiastically to his kissing, he tried sliding his hand up her blouse. Suddenly she jerked away, got out of the car and stomped home. That night she wrote in her diary, "A girl's best friends are her own two legs."

On their next date, Carl returned to the country road. As they were necking, he slid his hand up Mary's skirt. Once again, she pulled away, got out of the car and stomped home. That night she wrote in her diary, "I repeat, a girl's best friends are her own two legs."

On the third date, the pair returned to the country road. This time, Mary didn't get home until very late. That night she wrote, "Dear diary: There comes a time when even the best of friends must part."

A LETTER TO MY DEAR GIRLFRIEND, (G)

During the past year I have tried to make love to you 365 times. I have succeeded 36 times, which is an average of once every ten days. The following is a list of why I did not succeed more often:

    54 times the sheets were clean
    17 times it was too late
    49 times you were too tired
    20 times it was too hot
    15 times you pretended to be asleep
    2 times you had a headache
    17 times you were afraid of waking the children
    16 times you said you were too sore
    12 times it was the wrong time of the month
    19 times you had to get up early
    9 times you said you weren' in the mood
    7 times you were sunburned

      6 times you were watching the late show
      5 times you didn't want to mess up your new hairdo
      3 times you said the neighbors would hear us
      9 times you said your mother would hear us
Of the 36 times I did succeed, the activity was not satisfactory because:
      6 times you just laid there
      8 times you reminded me there's a crack in the ceiling
      4 times you told me to hurry up and get it over with
      7 times I had to wake you and tell you I finished
      1 time I was afraid I had hurt you because I felt you move

[Darwin Award Runner-Up] (G)

LOS ANGELES, CA. Ani Saduki, 33, and his brother decided to remove a bees' nest from a shed on their property with the aid of a pineapple. A pineapple is an illegal firecracker which is the explosive equivalent of one-half stick of dynamite. They ignited the fuse and retreated to watch from inside their home, behind a window some 10 feet away from the hive/shed. The concussion of the explosion shattered the window inwards, seriously lacerating Ani. Deciding Mr. Saduki needed stitches, the brothers headed out to go to a nearby hospital. While walking towards their car, Ani was stung three times by the surviving bees. Unbeknownst to either brother, Ani was allergic to bee venom, and died of suffocation enroute to the hospital.

Ultimate Disclaimer: (G)

This message does not reflect the thoughts or opinions of either myself, my company, my friends, or my cat; don't quote me on that; don't quote me on anything; all rights reserved; you may distribute this message freely but you may not make a profit from it; terms are subject to change without notice; illustrations are slightly enlarged to show detail; any resemblance to actual persons, living or dead, is unintentional and purely coincidental; do not remove this disclaimer under penalty of law; hand wash only, tumble dry on low heat; do not bend, fold, mutilate, or spindle; your mileage may vary; no substitutions allowed; for a limited time only; this message is void where prohibited, taxed, or otherwise restricted; caveat emptor; message is provided "as is" without any warranties; reader assumes full responsibility; an equal opportunity message; no shoes, no shirt, no message; quantities are limited while supplies last; if any defects are discovered, do not attempt to read them yourself, but return to an authorized service center; read at your own risk; parental advisory - explicit lyrics; text may contain explicit materials some readers may find objectionable, parental guidance is advised; keep away from sunlight; keep away from pets and small children; limit one-per-family please; no money down; no purchase necessary; you need not be present to win; some assembly required; batteries not included; instructions are included; action figures sold separately; no preservatives added; slippery when wet; safety goggles may be required during use; sealed for your protection, do not read if safety seal is broken; call before you dig; not liable for damages arising from use or misuse; for external use only; if rash, irritation, redness, or swelling develops, discontinue reading; read only with proper ventilation; avoid extreme temperatures and store in a cool dry place; keep away from open flames; avoid contact with eyes and skin and avoid inhaling fumes; do not puncture, incinerate, or store above 120 degrees Fahrenheit; do not place near a flammable or magnetic source; smoking this message could be hazardous to your health; the best safeguard, second only to abstinence, is the use of a condom; no salt, MSG, artificial color or flavoring added; if ingested, do not induce vomiting, and if symptoms persist, consult a physician; messages are ribbed for your pleasure; possible penalties for early withdrawal; offer valid only at participating sites; slightly higher west of the Rockies; allow four to six weeks for delivery; must be 18 to read; disclaimer does not cover misuse, accident, lightning, flood, tornado, tsunami, volcanic eruption, earthquake, hurricanes and other Acts of God, neglect, damage from improper reading, incorrect line voltage, improper or unauthorized reading, broken antenna or marred cabinet, missing or altered serial numbers, electromagnetic radiation from nuclear blasts, sonic boom vibrations, customer adjustments that are not covered in this list, and incidents owing to an airplane crash, ship sinking or taking on water, motor vehicle crashing, dropping the item, falling rocks, leaky roof, broken glass, mud slides, forest fire, or projectile (which can include, but not be limited to, arrows, bullets, shot, BB's, shrapnel, lasers, napalm, torpedoes, or emissions of X-rays, Alpha, Beta and Gamma rays, knives, stones, etc.); -and- other restrictions may apply!

WILL THE REAL DUMMY PLEASE STAND UP (G)

AT&T fired President John Walter after nine months saying he lacked intellectual leadership. He received a $26 million severance package. Perhaps it's not Walter who's lacking intelligence.

Blonde Joke (PG-13)

A woman's car breaks down on the Interstate, so the driver eases over onto the shoulder. She carefully steps out of the car and opens the trunk. Out jump two men in trench coats, who walk to the rear of the vehicle where they stand facing oncoming traffic and begin opening their coats and exposing themselves to approaching drivers. Not surprisingly, one of the worst pile-ups occurs. It's not very long before a police car shows up. The cop, clearly enraged, runs toward the driver of the disabled vehicle yelling, "What the hell is going on here?" "My car broke down," says the lady, calmly.

"Well, what are these perverts doing here by the road?" screams the cop.

"These are my emergency flashers!" replied the blonde!

How Information Travels (G)
MEMORANDUM

From: Executive Vice President, Headquarters - New York

To: General Managers

Next Thursday at 10:30 Halley's Comet will appear over this area. This is an event which occurs only once every 75 years. Notify all directors and have them arrange for all employees to assemble on the Company lawn and inform them of the occurrence of this phenomenon. If it rains, cancel the day's observation and assemble in the auditorium to see a film about the comet.

MEMORANDUM

From: General Manager

To: Managers

By order of the Executive Vice President, next Thursday at 10:30, Halley's Comet will appear over the Company lawn. If it rains, cancel the day's work and report to the auditorium with all employees where we will show films: a phenomenal event which occurs every 75 years.

MEMORANDUM
From: Managers
To: Section Chiefs
Next Thursday at 10:30 the Executive Vice President will appear in the auditorium with Halley's Comet, something which occurs every 75 years. If it rains, the Executive Vice President will cancel the comet and order us all out to our phenomenal Company lawn.

MEMORANDUM
From: Section Chief
To: All EA's
When it rains next Thursday at 10:30 over the Company lawn, the phenomenal 75 year old Executive Vice President will cancel all work and appear before all employees in the auditorium accompanied by Bill Halley and his Comets.

Traveling Angels (G)

Two traveling angels stopped to spend the night in the home of a wealthy family. The family was rude and refused to let the angels stay in the mansion's guest room. Instead the angels were given a space in the cold basement. As they made their bed on the hard floor, the older angel saw a hole in the wall and repaired it. When the younger angel asked why, the older angel replied...Things aren't always what they seem.

The next night the pair came to rest at the house of a very poor, but very hospitable farmer and his wife. After sharing what little food they had, the couple let the angels sleep in their bed where they could have a good night's rest. When the sun came up the next morning the angels found the farmer and his wife in tears. Their only cow, whose milk had been their sole income, lay dead in the field. The younger angel was infuriated and asked the older angel how could you have let this happen! The first man had everything, yet you helped him. The second family had little but was willing to share everything, and you let their cow die

"Things aren't always what they seem," the older ange lreplied. When we stayed in the basement of the mansion, I noticed there was gold stored in that hole in the wall. Since the owner was so obsessed with greed and unwilling to share his good fortune, I sealed the wall so he wouldn't find it. Then last night as we slept in the farmer's bed, the angel of death came for his wife. I told him to take the cow instead. Things aren't always what they seem. Sometimes this is exactly what happens when things don't turn out the way we think they should. If you have faith in God, just trust that every outcome is always to your advantage. You might not realize it until much later.

NOT THE SHARPEST KNIFE IN THE DRAWER!! (G)

In Modesto, CA, Steven Richard King was arrested for trying to hold up a Bank of America branch without a weapon. King used a thumb and a finger to simulate a gun but unfortunately he failed to keep his hand in his pocket.

Zoot Suit (G)

A man was looking for a job and he noticed that there was an opening at the local zoo. He inquired about the job and discovered that the zoo had a very unusual position that they wanted to fill. Apparently their gorilla had died, and until they could get a new one, they needed someone to dress up in a gorilla suit and act like a gorilla for a few days. He was to just sit, eat and sleep. His identity would be kept a secret of course. Thanks to a very fine gorilla suit, no one would be the wiser.

The zoo offered good pay for this job, so the man decided to do it. He tried on the suit and sure enough, he looked just like a gorilla. They led him to the cage; he took a position at the back of the cage and pretended to sleep. But after a while, he got tired of sitting so he walked around a little bit, jumped up and down and tried a few gorilla noises. The people who were watching him seemed to really like that. When he would move or jump around, they would clap and cheer and throw him peanuts. And the man loved peanuts. So he jumped around some more and tried climbing a tree. That seemed to really get the crowd excited. They threw more peanuts. Playing to the crowd, he grabbed a vine and swung from one side of the cage to the other. The people loved it and threw more peanuts.

Wow, this is great, he thought. He swung higher and the crowd grew bigger. He continued to swing on the vine, getting higher and higher and then all of a sudden, the vine broke! He swung up and out of the cage, landing in the lion's cage that was next door. He panicked. There was a huge lion not twenty feet away, and it looked very hungry. So the man in the gorilla suit started jumping up and down, screaming and yelling, "Help, help! Get me out of here! I'm not really a gorilla! I'm a man in a gorilla suit! Heeellp!"

The lion quickly pounced on the man, held him down and said, "Will you SHUT THE HELL UP! You're going to get both of us fired!!!"

[Darwin Award Runner-Up] (G)

Derrick L. Richards, 28, was charged in April in Minneapolis with third-degree murder in the death of his beloved cousin, Kenneth E. Richards. According to police, Derrick suggested a game of Russian roulette and put a semiautomatic pistol (instead of the more traditional revolver) to Ken's head and fired.

Why It's GREAT To Be A Guy... (PG-13)
Your ass is never a factor in a job interview.
Your orgasms are real......always.
Your last name stays put.
The garage is all yours.
Wedding plans take care of themselves.
You don't have to curl up next to a hairy ass every night.
Chocolate is just another snack.
You can be president.
You can wear a white shirt to a water park.
Foreplay is optional.
You never feel compelled to stop a friend from getting laid.
Car mechanics tell you the truth.
You don't give a rat's ass if someone notices your new haircut.
The world is your urinal.
Hot wax never comes near your pubic area.
You never have to drive to another gas station because this one's just too icky.
Same work... more pay.
Wrinkles add character.
You don't have to leave the room to make emergency crotch adjustments.
Wedding Dress $2000; Tux rental $100.
If you retain water, it's in a canteen.
People never glance at your chest when you're talking to them.
The occasional well-rendered belch is practically expected.
New shoes don't cut, blister, or mangle your feet.
Porn movies are designed with you in mind.
Not liking a person does not preclude having great sex with them.
Your pals can be trusted never to trap you with: "So, notice anything different?"
One mood, all the time.

Teacher's Gift (G)

It was at the end of the school year, and a kindergarten teacher was receiving gifts from her pupils. The florist's son handed her a gift. She shook it, held it overhead, and said, "I bet I know what it is. Some flowers." "That's right" the boy said, "but how did you know?" "Oh, just a wild guess," she said.

The next pupil was the sweet shop owner's daughter. The teacher held her gift overhead, shook it, and said, "I bet I can guess what it is. A box of sweets."

"That's right, but how did you know?" asked the girl.

"Oh, just a wild guess," said the teacher. The next gift was from the son of the liquor store owner. The teacher held the package overhead, but it was leaking.

She touched a drop of the leakage with her finger and touched it to her tongue. "Is it wine?" she asked.

"No," the boy replied, with some excitement.

The teacher repeated the process, taking a larger drop of the leakage to her tongue.

"Is it champagne?" she asked.

"No," the boy replied, with more excitement. The teacher took one more taste before declaring, "I give up, what is it?" With great glee, the boy replied, "It's a puppy!"

HMO Manager (G)

Two doctors and an HMO manager died and lined up at the pearly gates for admission to heaven. St. Peter asked them to identify themselves.

One doctor stepped forward and said, "I was a pediatric spine surgeon and helped kids overcome their deformities." St. Peter said, "You can enter."

The second doctor said "I was a psychiatrist. I helped people rehabilitate themselves." St. Peter also invited him in.

The third applicant stepped forward and said, "I was an

HMO manager. I helped people get cost-effective health care." St. Peter said, "You can come in, too." But, as the HMO manager walked by, St. Peter added, "You can stay three days. After that you can go to hell.

[Darwin Award Runner-Up] (PG-13)

PHILLIPSBURG, NJ. An unidentified 29 year old male choked to death on a sequined pastie he had orally removed from an exotic dancer at a local establishment. "I didn't think he was" going to eat it," the dancer identified only as "Ginger" said, adding "He was really drunk."

The Silver Ladle (PG-13)

An elderly priest invited a young priest over for dinner. During the meal, the young priest couldn't help noticing how attractive and shapely the housekeeper was.

Over the course of the evening he started to wonder if there was more between the elderly priest and the housekeeper than met the eye. Reading the young priest's thoughts, the elderly priest volunteered, "I know what you must be thinking, but I assure you, my relationship with my housekeeper is purely professional."

About a week later the housekeeper came to the elderly priest and said, "Father, ever since the young Father came to dinner, I've been unable to find the beautiful silver gravy ladle. You don't suppose he took it do you?" The priest said, "Well, I doubt it, but I'll write him a letter just to be sure." So he sat down and wrote: "Dear Father, I'm not saying that you 'did' take a gravy ladle from my house, and I'm not saying you 'did not' take a gravy ladle. But the fact remains that one has been missing ever since you were here for dinner."

Several days later the elderly priest received a letter from the young priest which read: "Dear Father, I'm not saying that you 'do' sleep with your housekeeper, and I'm not saying that you 'do not' sleep with your housekeeper. But the fact remains that if you were sleeping in your own bed, you would have found the gravy ladle by now."

THREE ARGUMENTS THAT JESUS WAS IRISH: (G)
1. He never got married.
2. He never held a steady job.
3. His last request was a drink.

THREE ARGUMENTS THAT JESUS WAS PUERTO RICAN: (G)
1. His first name was Jesus.
2. He was always in trouble with the law.
3. His mother didn't know who his father was.

THREE ARGUMENTS THAT JESUS WAS ITALIAN: (G)
1. He talked with his hands.
2. He had wine with every meal.
3. He worked in the building trades.

THREE ARGUMENTS THAT JESUS WAS BLACK: (G)
1. He called everybody brother.
2. He had no permanent address.
3. Nobody would hire him.

THREE ARGUMENTS THAT JESUS WAS CALIFORNIAN: (G)
1. He never cut his hair.
2. He walked around barefoot.
3. He invented a new religion.

AND FINALLY, THE PROOF THAT JESUS WAS JEWISH: (G)
1. He went into his father's business.
2. He lived at home until the age of 33.
3. He was sure his mother was a virgin, and his mother was sure He was God.

Junior Drives (G)
Junior had just earned his driver's license. To celebrate, the whole family trooped out to the driveway and climbed into the car for his inaugural drive. Dad headed to the back seat, directly behind the newly minted driver. "I'll bet you're back there to get a change of scenery after all those months of sitting in the front passenger seat teaching me how to drive," said the beaming boy to his old man. "Nope," came dad's reply,

"I'm gonna sit back here and kick the back of your seat while you drive, just like you've been doing to me for 16 years."

Stolen Stuff (R)
A man walks out of a bar, stumbling back and forth with a key in his hand. A Cop on the beat sees him, and approaches, "Can I help you, sir?"

"Yesssh! Ssssshomebody ssshtole my car!" the man replies.

The Cop asks, "Where was the car the last time you saw it?"

"It wassss at the end of thisss key!" the man replies. About that time the Officer looks down to see that the man's "thing" is hanging out of his fly for all the world to see. He asks the man, "Sir, are you aware that you are exposing yourself?"

The man looks down woefully and without missing a beat, moans "OHHH GOD.....they got my girlfriend too!!!"

[Darwin Award Runner-Up] (G)

MOSCOW, Russia-A drunk security man asked a colleague at the Moscow bank they were guarding to stab his bullet-proof vest to see if it would protect him against a knife attack. It didn't, and the 25-year-oldguard died of a heart wound. (It's good to see the Russians getting into the spirit of the Darwin Awards.)

CEO Problems (G)

A fellow had just been hired as the new CEO of a large high tech corporation. The CEO who was stepping down met with him privately and presented him with three numbered envelopes. "Open these if you run up against a problem you don't think you can solve," he said.

Well, things went along pretty smoothly, but six months later, sales took a downturn and he was really catching a lot of heat. About at his wits's end, he remembered the envelopes. He went to his drawer and took out the first envelope. The message read, "Blame your predecessor."

The new CEO called a press conference and tactfully laid the blame at the feet of the previous CEO. Satisfied with his comments, the press - and Wall Street - responded positively, sales began to pick up and the problem was soon behind him.

About a year later, the company was again experiencing a slight dip in sales, combined with serious product problems. Having learned from his previous experience, the CEO quickly opened the second envelope. The message read,

"Reorganize." This he did, and the company quickly rebounded.

After several consecutive profitable quarters, the company once again fell on difficult times. The CEO went to his office, closed the door and opened the third envelope.

The message said, "Prepare three envelopes."

The Lawyer and The Blonde (G)

A lawyer and a blonde are sitting next to each other on a long flight from LA to NY. The lawyer leans over to her and asks if she would like to play a fun game. The blonde just wants to take a nap, so she politely declines and rolls over to the window to catch a few winks. The lawyer persists and explains that the game is really easy and a lot of fun. He explains "I ask you a question, and if you don't know the answer, you pay me $5, and vice-versa."

Again, she politely declines and tries to get some sleep. The lawyer, now somewhat agitated, says, "Okay, if you don't know the answer you pay me $5, and if I don't know the answer, I will pay you $500!."

Figuring that since she is a blonde that he will easily win the match. This catches the blonde's attention and, figuring that there will be no end to this torment unless she plays, agrees to the game. The lawyer asks the first question. "What's the distance from the earth to the moon?" The blonde doesn't say a word, reaches in to her purse, pulls out a five dollar bill and hands it to the lawyer.

Now, it's the blonde's turn. She asks the lawyer: "What goes up a hill with three legs, and comes down with four?" The lawyer looks at her with a puzzled look. He takes out his laptop computer and searches all his references. He taps into the Airplane with his modem and searches the Net and the Library of Congress.

Frustrated, he sends E-mails to all his coworkers and friends he knows. All to no avail. After over an hour, he wakes the blonde and hands her $500. The blonde politely takes the $500 and turns away to get back to sleep.

The lawyer, who is more than a little miffed, wakes the blonde and asks, "Well, so what IS the answer!?" Without a word, the blonde reaches into her purse, hands the lawyer $5, and goes back to sleep.

Made in Japan (G)

There was a Japanese man who went to America for sightseeing. On the last day, he hailed a cab and told the driver to drive to the airport. During the journey, a Honda drove past the taxi. Thereupon, the man leaned out of the window excitedly and yelled, "Honda, very fast! Made in Japan!"

After a while, a Toyota sped past the taxi. Again, the Japanese man leaned out of the window and yelled, "Toyota, very fast! Made in Japan!"

And then a Mitsubishi sped past the taxi. For the third time, the Japanese leaned out of the window and yelled, "Mitsubishi, very fast! Made in Japan!" The driver was a little angry, but he kept quiet.

And this went on for quite a number of cars.

Finally, the taxi came to the airport. The fare was US$300.

The Japanese says, "Why so much?"

There upon, the driver yelled back, "Meter, very fast! Made in Japan!"

FEMALE SOFA (PG-13)

A 500 lb. woman from Illinois was examined in a hospital. During the examination, an asthma inhaler fell from under her armpit, a dime was found under one of her breasts and a remote control was found lodged between the folds of her vulva.

Computer Gender (G)

A marketing director for a prominent computer manufacturer was devising a new advertising campaign for his company. While researching consumer response to his product, he asked "Naval ships are commonly referred to as 'she' or 'her'.

What gender would you assign to your computer? Give four reasons to support your answer..."

A large group of women reported that the computers should be referred to in the masculine gender because:
1. In order to get their attention, you have to turn them on.
2. They have a lot of data, but are still clueless.
3. They are supposed to help you solve problems, but half the time they are the problem.
4. As soon as you commit to one, you realize that, if you had waited a little longer you could have had a better model.

The men, on the other hand, concluded that computers should be referred to in the feminine gender because:
1. No one but the Creator understands their internal logic.
2. The native language they use to communicate with other computers is incomprehensible to everyone else.
3. Even your smallest mistakes are stored in long-term memory for later retrieval.
4. As soon as you make a commitment to one, you find yourself spending half your paycheck on accessories for it.

The Mistress (G)

A husband and wife were having dinner at a very fine restaurant when this absolutely stunning young woman comes over to their table, gives the husband a big kiss, tells him she'll see him later, and walks away.

His wife glares at him and says, "Who was that??!!" "Oh," replies the husband, "that was my mistress." The wife says, "That's it; I want a divorce."

"I understand," replies her husband, "but, remember, if you get a divorce, there will be no more shopping trips to Paris, no wintering in the Caribbean, no Lexus in the garage, and no more country club. But the decision is yours."

Just then the wife notices a mutual friend entering the restaurant with a gorgeous woman. "Who"s that woman with Jim?" she asks. "That's his mistress," replies her husband. "Ours is prettier," says the wife.

Nixon and Clinton (G)
Nixon: Watergate
Clinton: Waterbed

Nixon: His biggest fear - the Cold War
Clinton: His biggest fear - a Cold Sore

Nixon: Worried about carpet bombs
Clinton: Worried about carpet burns

Nixon: His Vice President was a Greek
Clinton: His Vice President is a geek

Nixon: Couldn't stop Kissinger
Clinton: Couldn't stop kissing her

Nixon: Couldn't explain the 18 minute gap in the Watergate tape.
Clinton: Couldn't explain the 36-DD bra in his brief case

Nixon: His nickname was Tricky Dick
Clinton: same

Nixon: Known for campaign slogan "Nixon's The One"
Clinton: Known for women pointing at him saying, "He's the one!"

Nixon: Well acquainted with G. Gordon Liddy
Clinton: Well acquainted with the G Spot

Nixon: Took on Ho Chi Minh
Clinton: Took on Ho

Nixon: Talked about achieving peace with honor
Clinton: Talked about getting a piece while on her

First Night (PG-13)

A young couple were married, and celebrated their first night together, doing what newlyweds do, time and time again, all night long. Morning comes and the groom goes into the bathroom but finds no towel when he emerges from the shower. He asks the bride to please bring one from the bedroom. When she gets to the bathroom door, he opened the door, exposing his body for the first time to his bride where she sees all of him well.

Her eyes went up and down and at about midway, they stopped and stared, and she asked shyly, What's that?, pointing to a small part of his anatomy.

He, also being shy, thought for a minute and then said, Well, that's what we had so much fun with last night. And she, in amazement, asked, Is that all we have left?

Politically Correct Terms About Females (PG-13)

She does not: Get PMS...
    She becomes: HORMONALLY HOMICIDAL
She does not have: A Killer Body...
    She is: GEOMETRICALLY SUPERIOR

She is not: A Bad Cook...
    She is: MICROWAVE COMPATIBLE
She is not: A Bad Driver...
    She is: AUTOMOTIVELY CHALLENGED
She is not: Easy...
    She is: HORIZONTALLY ACCESSIBLE
She does not: Cut You Off...
    She becomes: HORIZONTALLY INACCESSIBLE
She is not: Hooked On Soap Operas...
    She is: MELODRAMATICALLY FIXATED
She does not: Wear Too Much Make-Up...
    She is: COSMETICALLY OVERSATURATED
She will never: Gain Weight...
    She will become: A METABOLIC UNDERACHIEVER
She is not: A Screamer Or Moaner...
    She is: VOCALLY APPRECIATIVE
She will never: Sag...
    She will become: GRAVITATIONALLY CHALLENGED

Two Parrots (PG-13)

A lady approaches her priest and tells him, "Father, I have a problem. I have two female talking parrots, but they only know how to say one thing."

"What do they say?" the priest inquired.

"They only know how to say, 'Hi, we're prostitutes. Want to have some fun?'"

"That's terrible!" the priest exclaimed, "but I have a solution to your problem. Bring your two female parrots over to my house and I will put them with my two male talking parrots whom I taught to pray and read the bible. My parrots will teach your parrots to stop saying that terrible phrase and your female parrots will learn to praise and worship."

"Thank you!" the woman responded.

The next day the woman brings her female parrots to the

priest's house. His two male parrots are holding rosary beads and praying in their cage. The lady puts her two female parrots in with the male parrots. Immediately, the female parrots say, "Hi, we're prostitutes, want to have some fun?"

One male parrot looks over at the other male parrot and exclaims, "Put the beads away. Our prayers have been answered!"

THE PERIOD (G)

A kindergarten class had a homework assignment to find out about something exciting and relate it to the class the next day. When the time came to present what they'd found, the first little boy called upon walked up to the front of the class and, with a piece of chalk, made a small white dot on the blackboard, then sat back down. Puzzled, the teacher asked him just what it was. "It's a period," said the little boy.

"Well, I can see that," she said, "but what is so exciting about a period?"

"Darned if I know," said the little boy, "But this morning my sister was missing one, Daddy had a heart attack, Mommy fainted, and the man next door shot himself."

Telephone Answering messages (G)

"Hi. I am probably home, I'm just avoiding someone I don't like. Leave me a message, and if I don't call back, it's you."

~~~~~~~~~~~~~~~

(Narrator's voice:) There Dale sits, reading a magazine. Suddenly the telephone rings! The bathroom explodes into a veritable maelstrom of toilet paper, with Dale in the middle of it, his arms windmilling at incredible speeds! Will he make it in time? Alas no, his valiant effort is in vain. The bell hath sounded. Thou must leave a message.

~~~~~~~~~~~~~~~~

"Hi! John's answering machine is broken. This is his refrigerator. Please speak very slowly, and I'll stick your message to myself with one of these magnets."

~~~~~~~~~~~~~~~~

"Hello, you are talking to a machine. I am capable of receiving messages. My owners do not need siding, windows, or a hot tub. Their carpets are always clean. They give to charity through their office & do not need any pictures taken. They believe the stock market is a random crapshoot, and the entire insurance industry is one huge scam perpetrated by Mafioso accountants. If you're still with me, leave your name and number and they will get back to you."

~~~~~~~~~~~~~~~~

"This is not an answering machine: this is a telepathic thought recording device. After the tone, think about your name, your reason for calling, & a number where you can be reached, & my owner will think about returning your call."

~~~~~~~~~~~~~~~~

"You're growing tired. Your eyelids are getting heavy. You feel very, sleepy now. You are gradually losing your willpower & your ability to resist suggestions. When you hear the tone you will feel helplessly compelled to leave your name, number, and a message."

~~~~~~~~~~~~~~~~

Hello, you've reached Jim & Sonya. We can't pick up the phone right now, because we're doing something we really enjoy. I like doing it up & down, & Sonya likes doing it left to right...real slowly. So leave a message, & when we're done brushing our teeth we'll get back to you."

Pickle Slicer (PG-13)

A man walks home from his job at the Pickle Factory very depressed and glum. His wife, noticing his mood asks him what's wrong. He replies "I have a terrible urge to put my p*n*s in the pickle slicer down at the Pickle Factory. I'm trying to fight it, but don't know if I can hold out much longer." His wife is horrified, and tells him not to even think of doing such a terrible thing. A few days pass, and again the man comes home very depressed and glum. His wife again asks him what's wrong. He replies "I still have this terrible urge to put my p*n*s into the pickle slicer down at the Pickle Factory, and I don't think I can hold out much longer."

His wife is again completely horrified, and again tells him to stop thinking about doing such an awful thing, and suggests professional help.

The next day, the man comes home early from the Pickle Factory. He is pale and walks very slowly. His wife, upon seeing him, rushes to him and asks why he is so pale and why he has come home so early. He replies "I couldn't resist any longer. I put my p*n*s in the pickle slicer down at the Pickle Factory. I got caught, and they fired me." His wife is aghast, but out of curiosity asks 'What happened to the pickle slicer?' "They fired her too..."

Couple Gave Counseling a Shot (G)

A husband and wife pulled guns on each other and shot it out at church during a marriage counseling session after he arrived late, drinking a beer. Both were wounded. With a beer in one hand and a gun in the other, Michael M. shot his wife as she tried to walk out of the meeting at St. James Episcopal Cathedral, their counselor said. A bleeding B. Martin pulled a pistol from her purse and shot her husband in the shoulder. The two took the gunbattle outside, where Bonnie Martin collapsed and was fired on again. Michael Martin allegedly hit his wife at least once more before he ran out of bullets. "They were arguing. It was your typical domestic dispute. Then the fireworks started. It's a good thing that he had been drinking because he could have hit her more," said the Rev. Bud S. He was a lousy shot."

The Polish Blonde (R)

A blonde went into a world wide message center to send a message to her mother overseas. When the man told her it would cost $150 she exclaimed, I don't have that kind of money, but I would do ANYTHING to get a message to my mother in Poland! The man arched an eyebrow, Anything? Yes, anything! the blonde promised. With that, the man said, Follow me.

He walked into the next room and ordered, Come in and close the door.

She did. He then said, Get on your knees. She did. Then he said, Take down my zipper. She did. He said, Go ahead...take it out. She took it out and grabbed hold of it with both hands. The man closed his eyes and whispered, Well....go ahead! The blonde slowly brought her lips closer, and while holding it close to her lips she said loudly, HELLO....MOM?

Two Drunks in a Skyscraper (G)

Two drunks are sitting in a 40th floor bar.

"You know the wind is blowing so hard that if you jump you will be blown back in the building on the 10th floor.

"That sounds crazy".

The first drunk says, "Watch me." He jumps and 10 minutes later he walks up the stairs into the bar. "That was great". Wanna try it?"

The second drunk says, "Is it really safe?"

"Sure. Watch me do it again". Sure enough he jumps again and walks back into the bar 10 minutes later. "A piece of cake", says the first drunk.

The second drunk jumps and goes straight down to the ground.

The bartender comes over and says to the first drunk, "Superman, you can be a real jerk sometimes".

A Little Too Strange (G)
Abraham Lincoln was elected to Congress in 1846.
John F. Kennedy was elected to Congress in 1946.
Abraham Lincoln was elected President in 1860.
John F. Kennedy was elected President in 1960.
The names Lincoln and Kennedy each contain seven letters.
Both were particularly concerned with civil rights.
Both their wives lost their children while living in the White House.
Both Presidents were shot on a Friday. Both were shot in the head.
Both were shot in the presence of their wives.
The Secretary of each President warned them not to go to the theater and to Dallas, respectively.
Lincoln's Secretary was named Kennedy.
Kennedy's Secretary was named Lincoln.
Both were assassinated by Southerners.
Both were succeeded by Southerners.
Both successors were named Johnson.
Andrew Johnson, who succeeded Lincoln, was born in 1808.
Lyndon Johnson, who succeeded Kennedy, was born in 1908.
John Wilkes Booth, who assassinated Lincoln, was born in 1839.
Lee Harvey Oswald, who assassinated Kennedy, was born in 1939.
Both assassins were known by their three names. Both names have 15 letters.
Booth ran from the theater and was captured in a warehouse.
Oswald ran from the warehouse and was captured in a theater.
To cap it all off, Booth and Oswald were assassinated before their trial.
What do you think: Mystery or a statistical coincidence?
I think it's an alien plot.

The 1999 Ferrari (G)
A hip young man goes out and buys the best car available: a 1999 Ferrari. It is also most expensive car in the world, and it

costs him $500,000.

He takes it out for a spin and stops for a red light. An old man on a moped (both looking about 90 years old) pulls up next to him. The old man looks over at the sleek, shiny car and asks, "What kind of car ya'got there, sonny?" The young man replies, "A 1999 Ferrari, it cost half a million dollars!" "That's a lot of money" says the old man. "Why does it cost so much?" "Because this car can do up to 320 miles an hour!" states the young man proudly. The moped driver asks, "Mind if I take a look inside?"

"No problem," replies the owner.

So the old man pokes his head in the window and looks around. Then, sitting back on his moped, the old man says, "That's a pretty nice car, all right!" Just then the light changes so the guy decides to show the old man just what his car can do. He floors it, and within 30 seconds the speedometer reads 210 mph.

Suddenly, he notices a dot in his rear view mirror. It seems to be getting closer!

He slows down to see what it could be and suddenly, whhoooossshhh! Something whips by him, going much faster! "What on earth could be going faster than my Ferrari?!" the young man asks himself.

Then, ahead of him, he sees a dot coming toward him. Whoooooosh! It goes by again, heading the opposite direction!

And it looked like the old man on the moped!

"Couldn't be!" thinks the guy. "How could a moped outrun a Ferrari?!" But again, he sees a dot in his rear view mirror! Whooooosh and KablaMMM!

It plows into the back of his car, demolishing the rear end. The young man jumps out, and it IS the old man!!! He runs up to the mangled old man and says, "Omigod! Is there anything I can do for you?"

The old man whispers in a raspy breath, "Unhook...my suspenders...from your side-view mirror..."

Two Sperms (R)
Two sperm swimming next to each other. One says to the other, "how long before we get to the egg?" To which the other sperm replies, "we haven't even made it passed the tonsils yet."

False Rumor (PG-13)
Way down south, there's a Baptist minister of a large congregation. One morning after a particularly moving sermon, he says, "Friends, I have been hearing nasty rumors!" The crowd falls into an expectant silence. "One of you, my faithful followers, has been saying that I am a member of the Klu Klux Klan. This is not true! I am now asking that the guilty party confess and apologize here before my flock."

Just then Sister Margaret stands up, "Preacher, I don't know how this came to be. All I said was that you're a wizard under the sheets."

DID I SAY THAT??? (G)
Police in Los Angeles had good luck with a robbery suspect who just couldn't control himself during a lineup. When detectives asked each man in the lineup to repeat the words, "Give me all your money or I'll shoot", the man shouted, "That's not what I said!"

Slogans for women's T-shirts
1. I'm out of estrogen - I have a gun
2. Guys have feelings too. But like... who cares?

3. Next mood swing: 6 minutes.
4. I used to be schizophrenic, but we're ok now.
5. Warning: I have an attitude and I know how to use it.
6. Of course I don't look busy...I did it right the first time.
7. I'm multi-talented: I can talk and annoy you at the same time.
8. I'm one of those bad things that happen to good people.
9. How can I miss you if you won't go away?
10. Sorry if I looked interested. I'm not.
11. Objects Under This Shirt Are Larger Than They Appear

Tiddles is Dead (R)

Little Lucy went out into the garden and saw her cat Tiddles lying on the ground with its eyes shut and its legs in the air. She fetched her Dad to look at Tiddles, and on seeing the cat he said, as gently as he could, "I'm afraid Tiddles is dead, Lucy".

"So why are his legs sticking up in the air like that, Daddy?"asked Lucy as she fought back the tears.

At a loss for something to say the father replied, 'Tiddles' legs are pointing straight up in the air so that it will be easier for Jesus to float down from heaven above and grab a leg and lift Tiddles up to heaven".

Little Lucy seemed to take her Tiddles death quite well. However, two days later when her father came home from work Lucy had tears in her eyes and said: "Mommy almost died this morning".

Fearing something terrible had happened the father shook the girl and shouted, "How do you mean Lucy? Tell Daddy!"
"Well", mumbled Lucy, "soon after you left for work this morning I saw mommy lying on the floor with her legs in the air and she was shouting, "Oh Jesus!!! I'm coming, I'm coming!!!" and if it hadn't been for the postman holding her down she would definitely have gone, Daddy".

Mike the Gorilla Lover (PG-13)

A certain zoo had acquired a very rare species of gorilla. Within a few weeks, the female gorilla became very ornery, and difficult to handle. Upon examination, the zoo veterinarian determined the problem. The gorilla was in heat. To make matters worse, there were no male gorilla species available.

While reflecting on their problem, the zoo administrators noticed Mike, an employee responsible for cleaning the animals' cages. Mike, it was rumored, possessed ample ability to satisfy any female, but he wasn't very bright. So, the zoo administrators thought they might have a solution.

Mike was approached with a proposition: would he be willing to screw the gorilla for five hundred bucks? Mike showed some interest, but said he would have to think the matter over carefully.

The following day, Mike announced that he would accept their offer, but only under three conditions. "First," he said, "I don't want to have to kiss her. Secondly, I want nothing to do with any offspring that may result from this union."

The zoo administration quickly agreed to these conditions, so they asked what was his third condition.

"Well," said Mike, "you've gotta give me another week to come up with the five hundred bucks."

Indian Name (PG-13)

This Indian boy goes to his mother one day with a puzzled look on his face. "Say, mom, why is my bigger brother named Mighty Storm?" She told him, "Because he was conceived during a mighty storm." Then he asked, "Why is my sister named Cornflower?" She replied, "Well, your father and I were in a cornfield when we made her."

"And why is my other sister called Moonchild?" The mother said, "We were watching the moon landing while she was conceived."

Mother Indian paused and asked her son, "Tell me, Torn Rubber, why are you so curious?"

The Shepherd and Ventriloquist (PG-13)

A ventriloquist who could throw his voice anywhere he wanted saw a shepherd on a hill with a dog, a mule, and a flock of sheep.

With all intentions of playing a joke he approached the shepherd and asked, "Hey mister does your dog talk?" the shepherd answered, "Hell no! Dogs don't talk!"

The ventriloquist threw his voice to the dog and said, "Yes I do you son of a bitch, all you do is kick me in the butt and you never feed me!" Hearing this the shepherd said, "I'll be damned!" The ventriloquist then asked, "How about that mule over there, does he talk?"

The shepherd replied, "Hell no mules don't talk!" Upon this reply the ventriloquist threw his voice towards the mule and said, "Yes I do you lowlife, all you do is burrow me down with weight, and pull my ears to get me to move!" The shepherd was astounded saying, "I can't believe this!"

Then the voice thrower asked, "How 'bout these sheep here, do they talk?"

The shepherd replied, "Yeah, but they're all a bunch of damn liars!"

Blonde Joke (R)

To prepare for his big date, the young man went up on to the roof of his apartment building in order to tan himself. Not wanting any tan lines to show, he sunbathed in the nude. Unfortunately, the young man fell asleep while on the roof, and managed to get a sunburn on his "tool of the trade." But the young man was determined not to miss his date, so he put some lotion on his manhood and wrapped it in gauze. The blonde showed up for the date at his apartment, and the young man treated her to a home-cooked dinner, after which they went into the living room to watch a movie. During the movie, however, the young man's sunburn started acting up again. He asked to be excused, went into the kitchen, and poured a tall, cool glass of milk. He then placed his sunburned member in the milk and experienced immediate relief of his pain.

The blonde, however, wondering what he was doing, wandered into the kitchen to see him with his Johnson immersed in a glass of milk. Upon seeing this, the blonde exclaimed, "So that's how you load those things!"

Female Comeback Lines (PG-13)

Man: "Haven't we met before?"
Woman: "Yes, I'm the receptionist at the VD Clinic."

Man: "Haven't I seen you someplace before?
Woman: "Yeah, that's why I don't go there anymore."

Man: "Is this seat empty?"
Woman: "Yes, and this one will be too if you sit down."

Man: "So, wanna go back to my place?"
Woman: "Well, I don't know. Will two people fit under a rock?"
Man: "Your place or mine?"
Woman: "Both. You go to yours and I'll go to mine."

Man: "I'd like to call you. What's your number?"
Woman: "It's in the phone book."
Man: "But I don't know your name."
Woman: "That's in the phone book too."

Man: "So what do you do for a living?"
Woman: "I'm a female impersonator."

Man: "What sign were you born under?"
Woman: "No Parking."

Man: "Hey, baby, what's your sign?"
Woman: "Do not Enter"

Man: "How do you like your eggs in the morning?"
Woman: "Unfertilized !"

Man: "Hey, come on, we're both here at this bar for the same reason."
Woman: "Yeah! Let's pick up some chicks!"

Man: "I'm here to fulfill your every sexual fantasy."
Woman: "You mean you've got both a donkey and a Great Dane?"

Man: "I want to give myself to you."
Woman: "Sorry, I don't accept cheap gifts."

Man: "Hey cutie, how 'bout you and I hitting the hot spots?"
Woman: "Sorry, I don't date outside my species.."

Man: "Your body is like a temple."
Woman: "Sorry, there are no services today."

Man: "I would go to the end of the world for you.
Woman: "Yes, but would you stay there?

Wild Woman (PG-13)

A woman entered a pawn shop and asked to see a pistol. She then asked for some bullets. Loading the gun, she ordered the pawnbroker to empty out the cash register. But then she said, "I have an even greater urge. Get into the back room!" There she ordered him to disrobe, and began having sex with him.

She got so involved that she dropped the gun.

"For God sakes, lady," the man said "pick it back up. My wife is due any time now!"

A whole lotto money (G)

Frank Capaci, 67, last weeks Powerball jackpot winner of $104.3 million isn't going to Disney World. After receiving an over-sized, ceremonial check at the news conference last week, Capaci stated: "I need a beer."

Capaci says he has no plans of quitting his part-time job mowing grass at the Hoffman Estates golf course, Chicago. "If those greens aren't mowed, the golfer's can't play," he said.

Among his first purchases, Capaci said, might buy a 95th anniversary Harley-Davidson motorcycle with a sidecar, a set of World War II goggles and helmet for his wife, and a new set of teeth.

Monkey Business (PG-13)

A police officer came upon a terrible wreck where the driver and passenger had been killed. As he looked upon the wreckage a little monkey came out of the brush and hopped around the crashed car. The officer looked down at the monkey and said "I wish you could talk."

The monkey looked up at the officer and shook his head up

and down.

"You can understand what I'm saying?" asked the officer.

Again, the monkey shook his head up and down.

"Well, did you see this?"

"Yes," motioned the monkey.

"What happened?"

The monkey pretended to have a can in his hand and turned it up by his mouth.

"They were drinking?" asked the officer.

"Yes."

"What else?"

The monkey pinched his fingers together and held them to his mouth.

"They were smoking marijuana?"

"Yes."

"What else?"

The monkey motioned "Screwing."

"They were screwing, too?" asked the astounded officer.

"Yes."

"Now wait, you're saying your owners were drinking, smoking and screwing before they wrecked."

"Yes."

"What were you doing during all this?"

"Driving" motioned the monkey.

Foreign Legion Recruit (PG-13)

The recruit had just arrived at a Foreign Legion post in the desert. He asked his corporal what the men did for recreation. The corporal smiled wisely and said, "You'll see." The young man was puzzled.

"Well, you've got more than a hundred men on this base and I don't see a single woman."

"You'll see," the corporal repeated.

That afternoon, three hundred camels were herded in the

corral. At a signal, the men seemed to go wild. They leaped into the corral and began to screw the camels.

The recruit saw the corporal hurrying past him and grabbed his arm. "I see what you mean, but I don't understand," he said.   "There must be three hundred of those camels and only about a hundred of us. Why is everybody rushing? Can't a man take his time?"

"What?" exclaimed the corporal, startled. "And get stuck with an ugly one?"

Great Business Idea (G)

Determined to reduce the number of disease-carrying insects, Manila officials offered a bounty of 1.50 pesos (6 cents) for every 10 cockroaches turned in. The Asahi Evening News reported the offer has given rise to a booming industry in the Philippines: roach farming.

Ghost Story (R)

1200 persons attended the recent International Paranormal Studies conference.

Moderator: "How many attendees believe in ghosts?" (Over 80% of the hands were raised)

Moderator: "How many have actually seen a ghost?" (58% of the hands were raised)

Moderator: "How many believe that a ghost can be solid?" (23% of the hands were raised)

Moderator: "How many have ever physically touched a ghost?" (3% of the hands were raised)

Moderator: "How many have ever had sex with a ghost?" (After some pause one lonely hand at the back of the hall went up)

Moderator: "May I ask where you are from, sir?"
Attendee: "I am from Talaine, Illinois."
Moderator: "And you say you've had sex with a ghost?"
Attendee: "Oh, I thought you said "goat."

Constipated Elephant (G)
PADERBORN, GERMANY –

Overzealous zookeeper Friedrich Riesfeldt fed his constipated elephant Stefan 22 doses of animal laxative and more than a bushel of berries, figs and prunes before the plugged-up pachyderm finally let fly -- and suffocated the keeper under 200 pounds of poop!

Investigators say ill-fated Friedrich, 46, was attempting to give the ailing elephant an olive-oil enema when the relieved beast unloaded on him like a dump truck full of mud. "The sheer force of the elephant's unexpected defecation knocked Mr. Riesfeldt to the ground, where he struck his head on a rock and lay unconscious as the elephant continued to evacuate his bowels on top of him," said flabbergasted Paderborn police detective Erik Dern. "With no one there to help him, he lay under all that dung for at least an hour before a watchman came along, and during that time he suffocated. "It seems to be just one of those freak accidents that happen."

Family Fun (PG-13)

One day John's tennis elbow was acting up and he decided to stop in and see a doctor. When he got to the doctor's office the nurse told him he could see the doctor in 15 minutes but, first he'd have to give a urine sample. John said that this was absurd but, the nurse insisted and John complied. 15 minutes later, John was ushered in to see the doctor.

"So that tennis elbow is really acting up, huh?" the doctor

said. "The nurse must have told you," said John, wondering how the Doctor knew. "No. It was in your urinalysis." and the doctor continued to say that he had just purchased this new machine that could diagnose every physical condition with total accuracy. John didn't believe a word of this but he did agree to provide another urine sample on check-up visit. Two days later, John was sitting at the kitchen table with his wife and his teen age daughter.

He was telling them about this ridiculous machine, when John decided to have a little fun with the doctor. John pissed in the bottle as did his wife and teen age daughter. Then while walking to his garage he had a brainstorm. John put a few drops of oil from his crankcase in the jar and finally beat off and put a few drops of semen in the jar. He drove to the doctors office, shook the bottle, then handed it to the nurse. This time his urinalysis took half an hour.

Finally, John was ushered in to see the doctor. The doctor looked at him and said, "I've got some bad news, smart ass. Your daughter is pregnant, your wife's got V. D., your car is about to throw a rod, and if you don't stop beating off that tennis elbow is never gonna heal!"

A Day in the Life (PG-13)

A doctor had come out of an examination room and begun to write a prescription. A nurse walked by and said, "Excuse me, Doctor, but you're trying to write with your thermometer." The doctor looked at the thermometer and said, "Dammit! Some asshole has my pen."

Octopus Talents (R)

A musical joke for all of you!

A guy walks into a bar with a octopus. He sits the octopus down on a stool and tells everyone in the bar that this is a very talented octopus. He can play any musical instrument in the world. He hears everyone in the crowd laughing at him, calling him an idiot, etc. So he says that he will wager $50 to anyone who has an instrument that the octopus can't play. A guy walks up with a guitar and sits it beside the octopus. The octopus starts playing better than Jimi Hendrix, just rippin' it up. So the man pays his $50. Another man walks up with a trumpet. The octopus plays the trumpet better than Dizzie Gillespie. So the man pays his $50. A third guy walks up with bagpipes. He sits them down and the octopus fumbles with it for a minute and sits it down with a confused look. "Ha!," the man says. "Can't you play it?" The octopus looks up at the man and says, "Play it? I'm going to f*ck it as soon as I figure out how to get its pajamas off."

Shock of a Lifetime (PG-13)

A man was experiencing chronic infections so he took his urologist's advice and entered the hospital for a routine circumcision. When he came to, he was perturbed to see a large group of doctors standing around his hospital bed.

"What's up doc?" he asked nervously.

"Uh, well......there's been a bit of a mix-up," admitted his surgeon. "I'm
afraid that instead of a circumcision, we performed a sex-change operation on you. You now have a very nice vagina instead of a penis."

"What!" gasped the patient. "You mean I'll never experience another erection?"

"Oh, I'm sure you *will*, reassured the doctor, "only it'll be somebody else's."

Underweight Baby (R)

The young lady entered the doctor's office carrying an infant. "Doctor," she explained, "the baby seems to be ailing. Instead of gaining weight, he lost three ounces this week." The medic examined the child and then started to squeeze the girl's breasts. He then unbuttoned her blouse, removed the bra and began powerfully sucking on one nipple. "Young lady," he finally announced, "no wonder the baby is losing weight, you haven't any milk!" "Of course not!" she shrieked. "It's not my child, it's my sister's!"

Dear Dr Ruth,

I'm writing to tell you my problem, It seems I have been married to a sex maniac for the past 22 years. He makes love to me regardless of what I am doing; Ironing, Washing dishes, Sweeping, even doing E-Mail on AOL, etc. I would like to know if there is anything that ucnn hlp m wth nd f unothel gothsl ehj fpslth fjsl;s;;o{O} .lp sldmpskdli dlks; a;ld;;'cinsely ous

---

A 90's Type of Woman (G)

A guy met this girl in a bar and asked, "May I buy you a drink?" "Okay. But it won't do you any good."

A little later, he asks, "May I buy you another drink?" "Okay. But it won't do you any good."

He invites her up to his apartment and she replies, "Okay. But it won't do you any good."

They get to his apartment and he says, "You are the most beautiful thing I have ever seen. I want you for my wife." She says, "Oh, that's different. Send her in."

THEY SAY THOSE THINGS WILL KILL YOU
[Darwin Award]

Not much was given to me on this unlucky fellow, but he qualifies nonetheless. You see, there was a gentleman from Korea who was killed by his cell phone... more or less. He was doing the usual "walking and talking" when he walked into a tree and managed to somehow break his neck.

Drunk at Church (PG-13)

A drunk staggered down the street and up the church steps. He managed to open the door and enter the silent building. On his hands and knees he struggled to the front of the church and finally made it into the confessional box.

Having observed the drunk's progress the priest sat silently in the booth, waiting for the drunk to speak. He waited for several minutes, hearing the drunk moan and groan, until finally there was a lengthy silence from the drunk's side of the confessional. At last the priest spoke. "May I help you my son?" he said.

"I don't know," the drunk replied. "It depends on whether or not you've got any paper on your side."

THUMB SUCKING (G)

A boy had reached four without giving up the habit of sucking his thumb, though his mother had tried everything from bribery to reasoning to painting it with lemon juice to discourage the habit. Finally she tried threats, warning her son that, "If you don't stop sucking your thumb, your stomach is going to blow up like a balloon." Later that day, walking in the park, mother and son saw a pregnant woman sitting on a bench. The 4-year-old considered her gravely for a minute, then spoke to her saying, "Uh-oh ... I know what you've been doing."

The Bond Between a Man and His Dog (R)

A woman has a dog who snores in his sleep and keeps her and her husband awake at night. She goes to the vet to see if he can help. The vet tells the woman to tie a ribbon around the dog's testicles and he will stop snoring. Of course the woman is very skeptical in believing this and goes home. A few hours after going to bed the dog is snoring as usual. Finally getting very frustrated, she goes tocloset and grabs a piece of ribbon, ties it around the dogs testicles, and sure enough the dog stops snoring. The woman is amazed.

Later that night her husband returns from being out with his friends and he is very drunk. He climbs into bed, falls asleep, and begins snoring very loudly.

The woman is desperate and thinks maybe the ribbon will work on him. She goes to the closet again, grabs a piece of ribbon, and ties it around her husbands testicles. Amazingly it also works on him. The woman falls asleep again and sleeps very soundly.

The next morning the husband wakes up very hung over. He stumbles into the bathroom to urinate. As he is standing in front of the toilet, he looks in the mirror and sees a blue ribbon attached to his scrotum. He is very confused. He walks back into the bedroom and sees a red ribbon attached to his dogs scrotum.

He looks at the dog and says "Boy, I don't remember what the hell happened last night, but where ever you and I where, we got first and second place."

Be Careful What You Wish For (PG-13)

A Man is walking down the beach and sees an old bottle in the sand and begins to play kick-the-bottle to amuse himself. After a while he picks it up, and a pissed off genie merges. She says "normally I grant 3 wishes, but in your case, you SOB, I am going to grant only 1."

He thinks a minute and says "OK, I want to wake up with 3 women in my bed."

She says "So be it!", and disappears back into the bottle.

Next morning, he wakes up with Lorena Bobbitt, Tonya Harding and Hillary Clinton. He has no penis, a broken leg, and no health insurance.

What They Been Thinking For Centuries (R)

For decades, two heroic statues, one male and one female, faced each other in a city park, until one day an angel came down from Heaven.

"You've been such exemplary statues," he announced to them, "that I'm going to give you a special gift. I'm going to bring you both to life for thirty minutes, in which you can do anything you want." And with a clap of his hands, the angel brought the statues to life.

The two approached each other a bit shyly, but soon dashed for the bushes, from which shortly emerged a good deal of giggling, laughter, and shaking of branches. Fifteen minutes later, the two statues emerged from the bushes, wide grins on their faces.

"You still have fifteen more minutes," said the angel, winking knowingly. Grinning even more widely, the female statue turned to the male statue and said,

"Great! Only this time YOU hold the pigeon down and I'LL shit on its head."

Is There No Justice (PG-13)

A husband and wife and their two sons are watching TV. She looks at her husband and winks at him, he gets the message and says, "Excuse us for a few minutes boys, we're going up to our room for a little while."

Pretty soon one of the boys becomes curious, goes upstairs and sees the door to his parents bedroom is ajar. He peeks in for a few minutes, trots downstairs, gets his little brother and takes him up to peek into the bedroom.

"Before you look in there," he says, "keep in mind this is the same woman who paddled our butts just for sucking our thumbs."

Uh-Oh (G)

There was a farmer who raised watermelons. He was doing pretty well, but he was disturbed by some local kids who would sneak into his watermelon patch at night and eat his watermelons. After some careful thought, he came up with a clever idea that he hopes will scare the kids away for sure: He makes up a sign and posts it in the field. That night the kids show up and see this sign which says,

"Warning: One of the watermelons in this field has been injected with cyanide."

The kids run off and make up their own sign which they post next to the farmer's sign. The next day, the farmer shows up to look over his field. He notices that no watermelons are missing but that there's now a sign next to his. He drives over to take a look. It says, "Now there are two."

Attorney Questions (G)

The following are questions actually asked of witnesses by attorneys during trials and, in certain cases, the responses given by insightful witnesses:

Q: Now doctor, isn't it true that when a person dies in his sleep, he doesn't know about it until the next morning?

Q: Were you present when your picture was taken?

Q: Was it you or your younger brother who was killed in the war?

Q: You were there until the time you left, is that true?

Q: How many times have you committed suicide?

Q: So the date of conception (of the baby) was August 8th?
A: Yes.

Q: And what were you doing at that time?

Q: You say the stairs went down to the basement?
A: Yes.

Q: And these stairs, did they go up also?

Q: Mr. Slatery, you went on a rather elaborate honeymoon, didn't you?
A: I went to Europe, Sir.
Q: And you took your new wife?

Q: Doctor, how many autopsies have you performed on dead people?
A: All my autopsies are performed on dead people.

Q: All your responses must be oral, OK? What school did you go to?
A: Oral.

Q: Do you recall the time that you examined the body?
A: The autopsy started around 8:30 p.m.
Q: And Mr. Dennington was dead at the time?
A: No, he was sitting on the table wondering why I was doing an autopsy.

Q: Are you qualified to give a urine sample?

You Can't Win (PG-13)
Bill and Linda decided that the only way to pull off a Sunday afternoon quickie with their ten-year-old son in the apartment was to send him out on the balcony and order him to report on all the neighborhood activities. The boy began his commentary as his parents put their plan into operation. "There's a car being towed from the parking lot," he said. "An ambulance just drove by." A few moments passed. "Looks like the Andersons have company," he called out, "Matt's riding a new bike and the Coopers are having sex." Mom and Dad shot up in bed. "How do you know that?" the startled father asked. "Their kid is standing out on the balcony too," his son replied.

The Closet (PG-13)
A married woman is having an affair. Whenever her lover comes over, she puts her nine year old son in the closet. One day the woman hears a car in the driveway and puts her lover in the closet, as well. Inside the closet, the little boy says, "It's dark in here, isn't it?"

"Yes it is," the man replies.

"You wanna buy a baseball?" the little boy asks.

"No thanks," the man replies.

"I think you do want to buy a baseball," the little extortionist continues.

"OK. How much?" the man replies after considering the position he is in.

"Twenty-five dollars," the little boy replies.

"TWENTY-FIVE DOLLARS?!" the man repeats incredulously, but complies to protect his hidden position.

The following week, the lover is visiting the woman again when she hears a car in the driveway and, again, places her lover in the closet with her little boy.

"It's dark in here, isn't it?" the boy starts off.

"Yes it is," replies the man.

"Wanna buy a baseball glove?" the little boy asks.

"OK. How much?" the hiding lover responds, acknowledging his disadvantage.

"Fifty dollars," the boy replies and the transaction is completed.

The next weekend, the little boy's father says "Hey, son. Go get your ball and glove and we'll play some catch."

"I can't. I sold them," replies the little boy.

"How much did you get for them?" asks the father, expecting to hear the profit in terms of lizards and candy.

"Seventy-five dollars," the little boy says.

"SEVENTY-FIVE DOLLARS?! That's thievery! I'm taking you to the church right now.

You must confess your sin and ask for forgiveness", the father explains as he hauls the child away. At the church, the little boy goes into the confessional, draws the curtain, sits down, and says "It's dark in here, isn't it?"

"Don't you start that in here," the priest says.

The Five Year Old (PG-13)
An old county doctor went way out to the boondocks to deliver a baby. It was so far out that there was no electricity. When the doctor arrived, no one was home except for the laboring mother and her 5 year old child

The doctor instructed the child to hold a lantern high so he could see while he helped the woman deliver the baby. The child did so, the mother pushed, and after a little while, the doctor lifted the new born baby by the feet and spanked him on the bottom to get him to take his first breath.

"Hit him again," the child said. "He shouldn't have crawled up there in the first place!!"

Kiss Me (G)
A boy was crossing a road one day when a frog called out to him and said, "If you kiss me, I'll turn into a beautiful princess." He bent over, picked up the frog and put it in his pocket. The frog spoke up again and said, "If you kiss me and turn me back into a beautiful princess, I will stay with you for one week."

The boy took the frog from out of his pocket, smiled at it and returned it to his pocket. The frog then cried out, "If you kiss me and turn me back into a princess, I'll stay with you and do *anything* you want." Again the boy took the frog out, smiled at it and put it back into his pocket. Finally the frog asked,

"What is it? I've told you I'm a beautiful princess, that I'll stay with you for a week and do *anything* you want. Didn't you hear me?" The boy said, "I heard ya! I'd just rather have a talking frog!"

Insurance Money (PG-13)

A woman recently lost her husband. She had him cremated and brought his ashes home. Picking up the urn that he was in, she poured him out on the counter...

Then she started talking to him, and tracing her fingers in the ashes, she said,

"You know that fur coat you promised me Irving?"

She answered by saying, "I bought it with the insurance money!"

She then said, "Irving, remember that new car you promised me?"

She answered again saying, "Well, I bought it with the insurance money!"

Still tracing her finger in the ashes, she said, "Irving remember that bj I promised you? Here it comes..."

[Darwin Award Runner-Up] (G)

In FRANCE, Jacques LeFevrier left nothing to chance when he decided to commit suicide. He stood at the top of a tall cliff and tied a noose around his neck. He tied the other end of the rope to a large rock. He drank some poison and set fire to his clothes. He even tried to shoot himself at the last moment. He jumped and fired the pistol. The bullet missed him completely and cut through the rope above him. Free of the threat of hanging, he plunged into the sea. The sudden dunking extinguished the flames and made him vomit the poison. He was dragged out of the water by a kind fisherman and was taken to a hospital, where he died of hypothermia.

REPUBLICANS RETHINK HMO LAWSUITS (G)

Some Republican House leaders changed their minds about letting patients sue HMOs after Republican Rep. Greg Ganske, a doctor, spoke in favor of it. He told of a young woman who fell 40 feet while mountain climbing. Her HMO refused to pay for her hospital stay because she didn't call ahead for prior authorization. Ganske said when she was lying at the bottom of the cliff, maybe she should've pulled out a cell phone with her one non-broken arm, called "Bambi" at the HMO, and said, "I have a broken skull. I need to go to the emergency room. Is that okay?"

"No! She should have gotten prior authorization BEFORE falling off the cliff!

"They would've said, "Okay, but no airlift! You'll have to hail a cab!"

Protecting the Trees (PG-13)

A lady from California purchased a piece of timber land in Oregon. There was a large tree on one of the highest points in the tract. She wanted to get a good view of her land so she started to climb the big tree. As she neared the top, she encountered a spotted owl that attacked her.

In her haste to escape, the lady slid down the tree to the ground and got many splinters in her private parts. In considerable pain, she hurried to the nearest doctor.

He listened to her story then told her to go into the examining room and he would see if he could help her. She sat and waited for three hours before the doctor reappeared.

The angry lady demanded "What took you so long?" and he replied "Well, I had to get permits from the Environmental Protection Agency, the Forest Service, and the Bureau of Land Management before I could remove old-growth timber from a recreational area."

Not Now (G)
Turkish Airlines fired pilot Altan Tezcan and co-pilot Erdogan Gecim, who were flying 240 passengers from Bangkok to Istanbul, after the two got into a fist fight in the cockpit while arguing over their aircraft's altitude.

Modern Age (PG-13)
Some people are sitting in a bar when one guy says, "My name is Larry, and I am a SNAG."

Another guy says, "What's that?"

The first guy says, "That means I am a Single, New Age Guy."

Another one says, "My name is Gary, and I am a DINK."

A girl asks, "What's that?"

He says, "That means I am a Double Income, No Kids."

A lady says, "That's nice. My name is Gertrude, and I am a WIFE."

Larry says, "A WIFE? What's a WIFE?"

She says, "That means, "Wash, Iron, F*ck, Etc."

Those Are Weapons (G)
Bernie Carson filed a $200,000 personal injury lawsuit against P.T.'s Show Club, claiming Busty Heart, a performer at the Bellevile, IL, strip club, caused him "emotional distress, mental anguish and indignity" when she slammed her large breasts into his neck and head. Carson also insisted he was "bruised, confused, lacerated and made sore" by Heart's 88-inch chest. Her breasts reportedly weigh 40 pounds each.

Embarrassing Moment (R)

In a Biology class, the professor was discussing the high glucose levels found in semen. A young female freshman raised her hand and asked, "If I understand, you're saying there is a lot of glucose, as in sugar, in male semen?"

"That's correct." responded the professor, going on to add statistical info. Raising her hand again, the girl asked, "Then why doesn't it taste sweet?" After a stunned silence, the whole class burst out laughing. The poor girl's face turned bright red, and as she realized exactly what she had inadvertently said, she picked up her books without a word and walked out of class.

The Lifesaver (PG-13)

A depressed young woman was so desperate that she decided to end her life by throwing herself into the ocean. When she went down to the docks, a handsome young sailor noticed her tears, took pity on her, and said, "Look, you've got a lot to live for. I'm off to Europe in the morning, and if you like, I can stow you away on my ship. I'll take good care of you and bring you food every day."

Moving closer, he slipped his arm around her shoulder and added, "I'll keep you happy, and you'll keep me happy." The girl nodded 'yes.' After all, what did she have to lose? That night, the sailor brought her aboard and hid her in a life-boat. From then on, every night he brought her three sandwiches and a piece of fruit, and they made passionate love until dawn.

Three weeks later, during a routine search, she was discovered by the captain. "What are you doing here?" the Captain asked. "I have an arrangement with one of the sailors," she explained. "He's taking me to Europe, and he's screwing me." "He sure is, lady," said the Captain. "This is the Staten Island Ferry."

Frightfully Sorry (G)
The Queen of England was showing the Archbishop of Canterbury around the Royal Stables when one of the stallions close by farted so loudly it couldn't be ignored.

"Oh dear," said the Queen, "How embarrassing. I'm frightfully sorry about that."

"It's quite understandable," said the archbishop, and after a moment added, "as a matter of fact I thought it was the horse."

Church Day (PG-13)
One bright Sunday morning Cindy and Mark took their eight year old son, Johnny, to church. They sat right in the front so Johnny could get all the benefits from church. But as we know eight year old boys do not like church at all. Especially little Johnny. Halfway through the pastor's sermon Johnny fell asleep. The pastor noticed this, and it was distracting him from preaching. He decided to go over to Johnny and ask him a question about God.

I "Son, do you know who created all the heavens and earth?"

His mother, Cindy, who did not want to be embarrassed by her son falling asleep, stuck a pin in her son's right butt cheek.

"GOD!!!!" Cried little Johnny.

"Very good," the pastor replied. For he could not say it was wrong. And he continued on. But a short while later, Johnny fell asleep again. The pastor once again noticed this and decided to ask another question "Who was Mary and Joseph's son?" The pastor asked. Johnny's dad, Mark, did not want to be embarrassed either, so he stuck a pin in his son's left butt cheek.

"JESUS CHRIST!!!!" Yelled Johnny.

And once again the pastor replied "Very good."

Near the end of the church service, Johnny could not control himself and fell asleep again. For the last time, the pastor decided to embarrass him and ask a very hard question. "What did Eve say to Adam on the morning when they woke up on the first day?"

But before Johnny's parents could do anything Johnny shouted "IF YOU STICK THAT THING IN ME ONE MORE TIME, I'M GOING TO TAKE IT AND BREAK IT IN HALF!"

GIMME A LIGHT! [Darwin Award]

In a west Texas town, employees in a medium-sized warehouse noticed the smell of gas. Sensibly, management evacuated the building, extinguishing all potential sources of ignition-lights, power, etc.

After the building had been evacuated, two technicians from the Gas Company were dispatched. Upon entering the building, they found they had difficulty navigating in the dark. To their frustration, none of the lights worked. Witnesses later described the vision of one of the technicians reaching into his pocket and retrieving an object that resembled a lighter. Upon operation of the lighter-like object, the gas in the warehouse exploded, sending pieces of it up to three miles away. Nothing was found of the technicians, but the lighter was virtually untouched by the explosion.

Why they call it Dope! (G)

Suspecting that a drug dealer might have sold her counterfeit crack cocaine, Rosie Lee Hill complained to Pensacola, FL, police. She was arrested after an investigating officer determined the two cocaine rocks were real. Hill said she had paid $50 for the drugs. But when she tasted them she thought they were baking soda.

Moose Call (G)

Two hunters went moose hunting every winter without success. Finally they came up with a foolproof plan. They got a very authentic cow moose costume and learned the mating call of a cow moose.

The plan was to hide in the costume, lure the bull, then come out of the costume and shoot the bull. They set themselves up on the edge of a clearing, donned their costume and began to give the moose love call.

Before long their call was answered as a bull came crashing out of the forest and into the clearing. When the bull was close enough, the guy in front said, "OK, lets get out and get him." After a moment that seemed like an eternity, the guy in the back shouted, "The zipper is stuck! What are we going to do!?" The guy in the front says, "Well, I'm going to start nibbling grass, but you'd better brace yourself"

College Rivalry (PG-13)

Three men were standing side-by-side using the urinal. The first man finished, zipped up and started washing and literally scrubbing his hands...clear up to his elbows....he used about 20 paper towels before he finished. He turned to the other two men and commented: I graduated from the University of Michigan and they taught us to be clean.

The second man finished, zipped up and quickly wet the tips of his fingers, grabbed one paper towel and commented: I graduated from the University of California and they taught us to be environmentally conscious.

The third man zipped up and as he was walking out the door said: I graduated from the University of Wyoming and they taught us not to piss on our hands.

Bad Bad Dog (R)

BREMERTON, WA - Christopher Coulter and his wife, Emily, were engaging in bondage games when Christopher suggested spreading peanut butter on his genitals and letting Rudy, their Irish Setter, lick them clean. Sadly, Rudy lost control and began tearing at Christopher's penis and testicles. Rudy refused to obey commands and a panicked Emily threw a half-gallon bottle of perfume at the dog. The bottle broke, covering the dog and Christopher with perfume. Startled, Rudy leaped back, tearing away the penis. While trying to get her unconscious husband in the car to take him to the hospital, Emily fell twice, injuring her wrist and ankle. Christopher's penis was in a Styrofoam ice cooler. "Chris is just plain lucky," said the surgeon who spent eight hours reattaching the penis. "Believe it or not, the perfume turned out to be very fortuitous. The high alcohol content, which must have been excruciatingly painful, helped sterilize the wound. Also, aside from its being removed, the damage caused by the dog's teeth to the penis per se is minimal. It's really a very stringy piece of flesh. Mr. Coulter stands an excellent chance of regaining the use of his limb because of this." Washington Animal Control has no plans to seize Rudy.

Good timing (G)

When Edmond James Ramos was charged with first-degree burglary in Los Angeles for breaking into an occupied dwelling, his lawyer appealed. He argued that because the only occupant had died of natural causes mere minutes before Ramos broke in, legally the residence was unoccupied. An appeals court agreed and threw out the charge.

Fresh Air (R)

A Chinese man arranges for a hooker to come to his room for the evening. Once in the room they undress, climb into bed, and go at it. When finished, the Chinese man jumps up, runs over to the window, takes a deep breath, dives under the bed, climbs out the other side, jumps back into bed with the hooker and commences a repeat performance. The hooker is impressed with the gusto of the second encounter. When finished, the Chinese man jumps up, runs over to the window, takes a deep breath, dives under the bed, climbs out the other side, jumps back into bed with the hooker and starts again. The hooker is amazed at this sequence. During the fifth encounter, she decides to try it herself. So when they are done she jumps up, goes to the window and takes a deep breath of fresh air, dives under the bed...and..... finds 4 Chinese men.

CLEANER POLISHES OFF PATIENTS
[Darwin Award] (G)

"For several months, our nurses have been baffled to find a patient dead in the same bed every Friday morning" a spokeswoman for the Pelonomi Hospital (Free State, South Africa) told reporters. "There was no apparent cause for any of the deaths, and extensive checks on the air conditioning system, and a search for possible bacterial infection, failed to reveal any clues." "However, further inquiries have now revealed the cause of these deaths... "It seems that every Friday morning a cleaning lady would enter the ward, remove the plug that powered the patient's life support system, plug her floor polisher into the vacant socket, then go about her business. When she had finished her chores, she would plug the life support machine back in and leave, unaware that the patient was now dead. She could not, after all, hear the screams and eventual death rattle over the whirring of her polisher". "We are sorry, and have sent a strong letter to the cleaner in question.

Further, the Free State Health and Welfare Department is arranging for an electrician to fit an extra socket, so there should be no repetition of this incident. The inquiry is now closed." (Cape Times).

Three Bullets (R)

A pregnant woman walks into a bank, and lines up at the first available teller. Just at that moment the bank gets robbed and she is shot three times in the stomach. She was rushed to the hospital where she was fixed up. As she leaves she asks the doctor about her baby.

The doctor says "Oh! You're going to have triplets. They're fine but each one has a bullet lodged in its stomach. Don't worry though the bullets will pass through their system through normal metabolism."

As time goes on the woman has three children. Two girls and a boy. Twelve years later, one of the girls comes up to her mother and says "Mommy, I've done a very weird thing!" Her mother asks her what happened and her daughter replies "I passed a bullet into the toilet".

The woman comforts her and explains all about the accident at the bank. A few weeks later, her other daughter comes up to her with tears streaming from her eyes. "Mommy, I've done a very bad thing!", the mother says "Let me guess. You passed a bullet into the toilet, right?". The daughter looks up from her teary eyes and says "Yes. How did you know?". The mother comforts her child and explains about the incident at the bank.

A month later the boy comes up and says "Mommy, I've done a very bad thing!".
"You passed a bullet into the toilet, right?"
"No, I was masturbating and I shot the dog"

Caught in the Cat Door (PG-13)

"In retrospect, I admit it was unwise to try to gain access to my house via the cat flap," Gunther Burpus admitted to reporters in Bremen, Germany. "I suppose that the reason they're called cat flaps, rather than human flaps, is because they're too small for people, and perhaps I should have realized that."

Burpus, a forty-one year old gardener from Bremen, was relating how he had become trapped in his own front door for two days, after losing his house keys.

"I got my head and shoulders through the flap, but became trapped fast around the waist. At first, it all seemed rather amusing. I sang songs and told myself jokes. But then I wanted to go to the lavatory. I began shouting for help, but my head was in the hallway so my screams were muffled.

After a few hours, a group of students approached me but, instead of helping, they removed my trousers and pants, painted my buttocks bright blue, and stuck a daffodil between my cheeks. Then they placed a sign next to me which said "Germany resurgent, an essay in street art. Please give generously' and left me there."

"People were passing by and, when I asked for help, they just said "very good! Very clever!" and threw coins into my trousers. No one tried to free me. In fact, I only got free after two days because a dog started licking my private parts and an old woman complained to the police. They came and cut me out, but arrested me as soon as I was freed. Luckily they've now dropped the charges, and I collected over DM3,000 in my underpants, so the time wasn't entirely wasted."

Q: Why are the flags at the Post Office at half staff?
A: They're hiring....

The Mystery (G)
A man walks into a pharmacy and asks for a pack of condoms. As soon as he has paid for them, he starts laughing and walks out.

The next day, the same performance, with the man walking out laughing, fit to bust. The pharmacist thinks this odd and asks his assistant, if the man returns, to follow him. Sure enough, he comes into the store the next day, repeating his actions once more. The assistant duly follows. Half an hour later, he returns.

"So did you follow him?"
"I did."
"And...where did he go?"
"Over to your house.."

Redneck Dating (Outside the Family) (G)
Always offer to bait your date's hook, especially on the first date.

Be aggressive. Let her know you are interested:
"I've been wanting to go out with you since I read that stuff on the men's bathroom wall two years a go."

If a girl's name does not appear regularly on a bathroom wall, water tower, or an overpass, odds are good that the date will end in frustration.

Captured by Indians (PG-13)
A cowboy is riding across the plains of the old west, when he is captured by Indians. The tribe puts him on trial for crimes against the Indian Nation, and he is found guilty.

"You have been sentenced to death," said the Chief, "but, as is our custom, you have three wishes to make as your last requests."

The cowboy thought for a minute and said, "Well, for my first wish, I'll need my horse."

"Give him his horse," said the Chief.

The cowboy whispered something into the horses ear, and the horse took off like a shot across the prairie.

Twenty minutes later, the horse returned with a beautiful blonde woman on its back. The cowboy looked at this, shrugged his shoulders, and helped the young lady off the horse. He then took her into the woods and had his way with her.

"Second wish," said the Chief.

"I'll need my horse again," said the cowboy.

Once again, the cowboy whispered into the horse's ear, and once again the horse rode off over the prairie.

Thirty minutes later, the horse returned with a beautiful redhead on its back. The cowboy looked up and shrugged, helped the young lady off the horse, and went into the woods.

"This is your last wish," said the Chief," make it a good one." The cowboy grabbed each side of the horse's head, and put his face right up to the horse's nose.

"I SAID POSSE!!!!!!!"

Automobile Acronyms (G)
AUDI - Accelerates Under Demonic Influence
BMW - Bought My Wife
BUICK - Big Ugly Indestructible Car Killer
CHEVROLET - Can Hear Every Valve Rap On Long Extended Trips
DODGE - Drips Oil, Drops Grease Everywhere
FIAT - Fix It All the Time
FORD - Fast Only Rolling Downhill (Also, Fix or Repair Daily)
GM - General Maintenance
GMC - Gotta Mechanic Coming?
HONDA - Had One Never Did Again

HYUNDAI - Hope You Understand Nothing's Driveable And Inexpensive...
MAZDA - Most Always Zipping Dangerously Along
OLDSMOBILE - Overpriced, Leisurely Driven Sedan Made Of Buic's Irregular Leftover Equipment
SAAB - Swedish Automobiles Always Breakdown
TOYOTA - Too Often Yankees Overprice This Auto
VOLVO - Very Odd Looking Vehicular Object
VW - Virtually Worthless

The Boss's Jokes (G)

The boss returned from lunch in a good mood and called the whole staff in to listen to a couple of jokes he had picked up. Everybody but one girl laughed uproariously. "What's the matter?" grumbled the boss. "Haven't you got a sense of humor?" "I don't have to laugh," she said. I'm leaving Friday."

A Little Late (G)

Shulamit D., 82, passed her driver's test in Ashdod, Israel, after 35 failures. She originally wanted her license so she could visit her parents in Tel Aviv, but she took so long that they died first.

Union Shop (R)

A dedicated shop steward was at a convention in Las Vegas and decided to check out the local brothels. When he got to the first one, he asked the madame, "Is this a union house?" "No, I'm sorry, it isn't," said the madame.

"Well, if I pay you $100, what cut do the girls get?" he

asked.

"The house gets $80 and the girl gets $20." Mightily offended at such unfair dealings, the man stomped off down the street in search of a more equitable shop. At the second one, he asked the madame, "Is this a union house?"

"No, I'm sorry, it isn't," said the madame.

"If I pay you $100, what cut do the girls get?" he asked again.

"The house gets $80 and the girl gets $20." Again offended, the man stomped off down the street in search of a more equitable shop. His search continued until he finally reached a brothel where the madame said, "Why yes, this is a union house."

"And if I pay you $100, what cut do the girls get?" he questioned. "The girls get $80 and the house gets $20."

"That's more like it!" the man said. He looked around the room and pointed to a stunningly attractive redhead. "I'd like her for the night." "I'm sure you would, sir", said the madame while gesturing to a grotesque woman in her seventies in the corner, "But Ethel here has seniority."

Superbowl Tickets (G)

There was this man who won a contest and got one free ticket to the Superbowl. He was so happy, but when he got to the stadium and found his seat he was somewhat disappointed. His ticket was for the last row, and it was WAY up there.' He couldn't see the game, so he began looking around. Close to the field he saw an empty seat, so he decided to go down there.

He reached the seat and asked the man next to the unoccupied seat if anyone was seating there.

The man replied, "No." So the guy sat down and struck up a conversation.

"Who would have a seat right next to the field and not come?!?" The man answers, "Oh, that was my wife's seat."
"Where is she?" the guy replied. "She died."
"Oh I'm sorry...don't you have anyone else to come with you, a brother, or friend?"
"No, they couldn't come."
"Why?"
"Because they are at her funeral."

OW OW OW   OUCH (PG-13)
LOS ANGELES, CA - Attorney Antonio M., was released from a trauma center after having a cell phone removed from his rectum. "My dog drags the thing all over the house," he said later. "He must have dragged it into the shower. slipped on the tile, tripped against the dog and sat down right on the thing."

The extraction took more than three hours due to the fact that the cover to Mr. Mendoza's phone had opened during insertion. "He was a real trooper during the entire episode," said Dr. Dennis Crobe. "Tony just cracked jokes and really seemed to be enjoying himself. Three times during the extraction his phone rang and each time, he made jokes about it that just had us rolling on the floor. By the time we finished, we really did expect to find an answering machine in there."

The Pumpkin Hour (PG-13)
So ol' Billy Bob gets all decked out for the barn dance (even changes his underwear) and off he goes. To his dismay upon arrival, he doesn't spot any single women so decides to get inebriated.

As he stumbles out the door to go home, he passes by a

pumpkin patch. The shapes of the pumpkins lit up by the full moon reminds him of curvaceous posteriors of women and gets him quite horny. In his drunken state of mind, he decides to relieve his amorous desire by dropping his drawers and starts humping one of the pumpkins. At that moment, a cop walks by and, seeing him, yells, "Hey Buddy!! Whaddya think yer doin' with that pumpkin!?"

Billy Bob stops, thinks for a moment, and then says, "Pumpkin? Sheesh, you mean to tell me that it's past midnight already!?"

Ultimate Computer (G)

The Ultimate Computer stood at the end of the Ultimate Computer Company's production line. At which point the guided tour eventually arrived. The salesman stepped forward to give his prepared demo. "This", he said, "is the Ultimate Computer. It will give an intelligent answer to any question you may care to ask it." At which a Clever Dick stepped forward - there is always one - and spoke into the Ultimate Computer's microphone. "Where is my father?" he asked. There was a whirring of wheels and flashing of lights that the manufacturers always use to impress lay people, and then a little card popped out. On it were printed the words "Fishing off Florida". Clever Dick laughed. "Actually", he said, "my father is dead!" It had been a tricky question!!

The salesman, carefully chosen for his ability to think fast on his feet, immediately replied that he was sorry the answer was unsatisfactory, but as computers were precise, perhaps he might care to rephrase his question and try again?

Clever Dick thought, went to the Ultimate Computer and this time said, "Where is my mother's husband?" Again there was a whirring of wheels and a flashing of lights. And again a little card popped out. Printed on it were the words:

"Dead. But your father is still fishing off Florida."

The Last Big War (PG-13)
A reporter was interviewing an old Scandinavian fighter pilot, asking him how it was in the war.

"Vell," said the old guy, "vee used to fly up dere and dogfight dem Krauts. Ya, vee used to shoot dem German fokkers outta da sky." "For the benefit of our viewers," interrupted the reporter, "we should explain that the term 'fokker' refers to a specific type of German fighter plane."

"Vell .ya," said the old Scandinavian pilot, "but those fokkers were Messerschmitt's."

My Best Friend (PG-13)
All the good knights were leaving for the Crusades. One knight told his best friend "My bride is without doubt one of the most beautiful women in the world. It would be a terrible waste if no man could have her. Therefore, as my best and most trusted friend, I am leaving you the key to her chastity belt to use should I not return from the Crusade."

The company of knights were only a mile or so out of town when they noticed a cloud of dust approaching. Thinking it might be an important message from the town the column halted. A horseman approached. It was the knight's best friend. He said " Hey, you gave me the wrong key!!"

Good News, Bad News (G)
One Sunday morning George burst into the living room and said, "Dad! Mom! I have some great news for you! I am getting married to the most beautiful girl in town. She lives a block away and her name is Susan.

"After dinner, George's dad took him aside, "Son, I have to talk with you. Look at your mother, George. She and I have been married 30 years. She's a wonderful wife and mother, but, she has never offered much excitement in the bedroom, so ... I used to fool around with women a lot. Susan is actually your half sister, and I'm afraid you can't marry her." George was broken-hearted.

After eight months he eventually started dating girls again. A year later he came home and very proudly announced, "Mom, Dad ... Dianne said yes! We're getting married in June." Again his father insisted on another private conversation and broke the sad news. "Dianne is your half sister too, George. I'm awfully sorry about this." George was livid! He finally decided to go to his mother with the news his father had shared. "Dad has done so much harm. I guess I'm never going to get married," he complained. "Every time I fall in love, Dad tells me the girl is my half sister."

"Heh heh," his mother chuckled, shaking her head, "Don't pay any attention to what he says. He's not really your father."

Darwin Award Candidate (G)
Man Loses Face at Party.

A man at a West Virginia party popped a blasting cap into his mouth and bit down, triggering an explosion that blew off his lips, teeth and tongue, state police said Wednesday. Jerry S., 24, of Kincaid, bit the blasting cap as a prank during a party late

Tuesday night, said Cpt. Payne. "Another man had it in an aquarium, hooked to a battery, and was trying to explode it," Payne said. "It wouldn't go off and this guy said, 'I'll show you how to set it off.

He put it in his mouth and bit down. It blew all his teeth off, his tongue and his lips," Payne said. Jerry was listed in guarded condition Wednesday with extensive facial injuries, according to a spokesman at Charleston Area Medical Division. "I just can't imagine anyone doing something like that," Payne said.

Taco Bell Dog (R)

This guy wakes up one morning to find a gorilla in his backyard tree. He gets his phone book to look up a gorilla removal service in the yellow pages. The gorilla service guy says he can help him out but he needs to know if its a male or female gorilla.

The man runs outside, checks it out and tells the service guy its a male gorilla. The service guy says, "OK, I'll be right over."

A short time later the service guy shows up with a stick, a Chihuahua, a shotgun, and a pair of handcuffs. He then gives the man some instructions: "Now, I'm going to climb this tree and poke the gorilla with the stick until he falls. When he does, the trained Chihuahua will attack the gorilla's testicles. The gorilla will then reach for his testicles to protect himself and that's when you snap the handcuffs on him."

"OK, the man says, but what do I do with the shotgun?" The service guy replies, "If I fall out of the tree before the gorilla, shoot the Chihuahua."

How Not to Save Face (G)

Everyone farts, admit it or not. Kings fart, Queens fart. Edward Lear, the 19th century English landscape painter, wrote affectionately of a favorite Duchess who gave enormous dinner parties attended by the cream of society. One night she let out a ripper and quick as a flash she turned her gaze to her stoic butler, standing, as always, behind her.

"Hawkins!" she cried, "Stop that!"

"Certainly, your Grace.", he replied with unhurried dignity, "Which way did it go?"

Life In Russia (G)

Morris, a Russian man saves his rubles for twenty years to buy a new car. After choosing the model and options he wants, he's not the least bit surprised or even concerned to learn that it will take two years for the new car to be delivered.

He thanks the salesman and starts to leave, but as he reaches the door he pauses and turns back to the salesman "Do you know which week two years from now the new car will arrive?" he asks. The salesman checks his notes and tells the man that it will be two years to the exact week. The man thanks the salesman and starts out again, but upon reaching the door, he turns back again.

"Could you possibly tell me what day of the week two years from now the car will arrive?"

The salesman, mildly annoyed, checks his notes again and says that it will be exactly two years from this week, on Thursday. Morris thanks the salesman and once again starts to leave. Halfway though the door, he hesitates, turns back, and walks up to the salesman.

"I'm sorry to be so much trouble, but do you know if that will be two years from now on Thursday in the morning, or in the afternoon?"

Visibly irritated, the salesman flips through his papers yet another time and says sharply that it will be in the afternoon, two years from now on Thursday.

"That's a relief!" says Morris. "The plumber is coming that morning!"

Modern Life (G)

A guy got a credit card bill stating that he owed $0.00. He ignored it and threw it away..

Next month he got another, did the same thing. The next month they sent him a very nasty note stating they were going to cancel his credit card if he didn't send them $0.00. He called them, talked to them, they said it was "a glitch" and told him they'd take care of it..

The following month he tried to charge something and couldn't. He called the credit card company who again said they'd take care of it.. The next day he got his bill for $0.00 stating that he was very delinquent.. The man figured the credit card company would take care of it, so he didn't worry. The next month he got a bill for $0.00 stating that he had 10 days to pay or his account was going to collection..

He mailed the credit card company a check for $0.00, and the credit card company's computer processed it, noting that his account was now paid in full..

A week later, the man's bank called him asking him what he was doing writing a check for $0.00. He explained and they said, "Well, your $0.00 check has caused our check processing software to fail. We now can't process ANY of our checks from that day electronically because that $0.00 check is causing the program to abort."

The man, who had been considering buying his wife a computer for her birthday, bought her a typewriter instead..

The Ugly Suit (G)

When the store manager returned from lunch, he noticed his clerk's hand was bandaged, but before he could ask about the bandage, the clerk said he had some very good news for him. "Guess what, sir?" the clerk said. "I finally sold that terrible, ugly suit we've had so long!"

"Do you mean that repulsive pink-and-blue double-breasted thing?" the manager asked.

"That's the one!"

"That's great!" the manager cried, "I thought we'd never get rid of that monstrosity! That had to be the ugliest suit we've ever had! But tell me. Why is your hand bandaged?"

"Oh," the clerk replied, "after I sold the guy that suit, his guide dog bit me."

Southern California Driver's License Application:

Name: _____ Stage name: _____

Agent: _____ Attorney: _____

Publicist _____ Manicurist/Hair stylist _____

Sex: __ male __ female __ formerly male __ formerly female __ both __

If female, indicate breast implant size: ____

Will the size of your implants hinder your ability to safely operate a motor vehicle in any way?   Yes ___ No ___

Occupation:
☐ Lawyer
☐ Actor/Waiter
☐ Filmmaker/Self-employed
☐ Writer
☐ Car Dealer
☐ Panhandler
☐ Agent
☐ Hooker/Transvestite
☐ Other; please explain: _____

Please check hair color:
Females: ☐ Blonde ☐ Platinum Blonde ☐ Ash Blonde
Teenagers: ☐ Purple ☐ Blue ☐ Green
Skinhead Men: Please list shade of hair plugs.

Please check activities you perform while driving:
(Check all that apply)
☐ Eating a wrap

☐ Applying make-up
☐ Talking on the phone
☐ Slapping kids in the back seat
☐ Having sex
☐ Applying cellulite treatment to thighs
☐ Tanning
☐ Snorting cocaine
☐ Watching TV
☐ Reading Variety
☐ Surfing the Net via your laptop

Please indicate how many times:
    a) you expect to shoot at other drivers ____
    b) how many times you expect to be shot at while driving ____

If you are the victim of a car-jacking, you should immediately:
    a) Call the police to report the crime;
    b) Call Channel 4 News to report the crime, then watch your car on the news on a high-speed chase;
    c) Call your attorney and discuss lawsuit against cellular phone company for 911 call not going through;

In the event of an earthquake, should you:
    a) stop your car,
    b) keep driving and hope for the best,
    c) immediately use your cell phone to call all loved ones, or
    d) pull out your video camera and obtain footage for TV

In the instance of rain, you should:
    a) never drive over 5 MPH,
    b) drive twice as fast as usual, or
    c) you're not sure what "rain" is.

Are you presently taking any of the following medications?
    a) Prozac;
    b) Zovirax;

c) Lithium;
d) Zantax;
e) Viagra.
If none, please explain: _____.

Length of daily commute:
a) 1 hour;
b) 2 hours;
c) 3 hours;
d) 4 hours or more.

New Business Venture (R)

A husband and wife were having difficulty surviving financially so they decided that the wife should try prostitution as an extra source of income. The husband drove her out to a popular corner and informed her he would be at the side of the building if she had any questions or problems.

A gentleman pulled up shortly after and asked her how much to go all the way. She told him to wait a minute and ran around the corner to ask her husband. The husband told her to tell the client $100. She went back and informed the client at which he cried "That's too much!" He then asked "How much for a handjob?" She asked him to wait a minute and ran to ask her husband how much. The husband said "Ask for $40." The woman ran back and informed the client.

He felt that this was an agreeable price and began to remove his pants and underwear. Upon the removal of his clothing the woman noticed that the man was well hung. She asked him once more to wait a moment. She ran around the corner again at which her husband asked "Now what?"

The wife replied "Can I borrow $60?"

IQ Test (G)
READ this sentence:
FINISHED FILES ARE THE RESULT OF YEARS OF SCIENTIFIC STUDY COMBINED WITH THE EXPERIENCE OF YEARS.
Now count ALOUD the F's in that sentence. Count them ONLY ONCE; do not go back and count them again. See below...

ANSWER: There are six F's in the sentence. One of average intelligence finds three of them. If you spotted four, you're above average. If you got five, you can turn your nose at most anybody. If you caught six, you are a genius. There is no catch. Many people forget the OFs. The human brain tends to see them as "V's" instead of "F's".

21st Century Science (G)
GRAND PRIZE WINNER: When a cat is dropped, it always lands on its feet, and when toast is dropped, it always lands with the buttered side facing down. I propose to strap buttered toast to the back of a cat; the two will hover, spinning inches above the ground. With a giant buttered cat array, a high-speed monorail could easily link New York with Chicago.

The maker doesn't want it; the buyer doesn't use it; and the user doesn't see it. What is it?
A. A coffin

It Never Stops (G)
A Jewish lady named Mrs. Rosenberg who many years ago was stranded late one night at a fashionable resort - one that did not admit Jews. The desk clerk looked down at his book and said, "Sorry, no room. The hotel is full." The Jewish lady

said, "But your sign says that you have vacancies." The desk clerk stammered and then said curtly, "You know that we do not admit Jews. Now if you will try the other side of town..."

Mrs. Rosenberg stiffened noticeable and said, "I'll have you know I converted to your religion." The desk clerk said, "Oh, yeah, let me give you a little test. How was Jesus born?"Mrs. Rosenberg replied, "He was born to a virgin named Mary in a little town called Bethlehem."

"Very good," replied the hotel clerk. "Tell me more."
Mrs. Rosenberg replied, "He was born in a manger."

"That's right," said the hotel clerk. "And why was he born in a manger?"

Mrs. Rosenberg said loudly, "Because a jerk like you in the hotel wouldn't give a Jewish lady a room for the night!"

My Breakfast Order (G)

A resident in a seaside hotel breakfast room called over the head waiter one morning and said, "I want two boiled eggs, one of them so undercooked it's runny, and the other so over cooked it's tough and hard to eat. Also grilled bacon that has been left on the plate to get cold; burnt toast that crumbles away as soon as you touch it with a knife; butter straight from the deep freeze so that it's impossible to spread; and a pot of very weak coffee, luke-warm."

"That's a complicated order sir," said the bewildered waiter. "It might be quite difficult." The guest replied, "Oh, but that's what you gave me yesterday!"

Marketing Slogans Gone Bad (G)

Coors put its slogan, "Turn it loose," into Spanish, where it was read as "Suffer from diarrhea."

Clairol introduced the "Mist Stick," a curling iron, into German only to find out that "mist" is slang for manure. Not too many people had use for the "manure stick".

Scandinavian vacuum manufacturer Electrolux used the following in an American campaign: Nothing sucks like an Electrolux.

When Gerber started selling baby food in Africa, they used the same packaging as in the US, with the beautiful baby on the label. Later they learned that in Africa, companies routinely put pictures on the label of what's inside, since most people can't read English.

Colgate introduced a toothpaste in France called Cue, the name of a notorious porno magazine.

An American T-shirt maker in Miami printed shirts for the Spanish market which promoted the Pope's visit. Instead of "I saw the Pope" (el Papa), the shirts read "I saw the potato" (la papa).

In Italy, a campaign for Schweppes Tonic Water translated the name into "Schweppes Toilet Water."

Pepsi's "Come alive with the Pepsi Generation" translated into "Pepsi brings your ancestors back from the grave," in Chinese.

Frank Perdue's chicken slogan, "it takes a strong man to make a tender chicken" was translated into Spanish as "it takes an aroused man to make a chicken affectionate."

When Parker Pen marketed a ball-point pen in Mexico, its ads were supposed to have read, "it won't leak in your pocket and embarrass you". Instead, the company thought that the word "embarazar" (to impregnate) meant to embarrass, so the ad read: "It won't leak in your pocket and make you pregnant".

Don't Worry (G)

While cruising at 40,000 feet, the airplane shuddered and Mr. Benson looked out the window.

"Good lord!" he screamed, "one of the engines just blew up!" Other passengers left their seats and came running over; suddenly the aircraft was rocked by a second blast as yet another engine exploded on the other side.

The passengers were in a panic now, and even the stewardesses couldn't maintain order. Just then, standing tall and smiling confidently, the pilot strode from the cockpit and assured everyone that there was nothing to worry about. His words and his demeanor seemed to make most of the passengers feel better, and they sat down as the pilot calmly walked to the door of the aircraft. There, he grabbed several packages from under the seats and began handing them to the flight attendants.

Each crew member attached the package to their backs.

"Say," spoke up an alert passenger, "aren't those parachutes?" The pilot said they were.

The passenger went on, "But I thought you said there was nothing to worry about?"

"There isn't," replied the pilot as a third engine exploded. "We're going to get help."

First Argument (G)

Sometimes women are overly suspicious of their husbands. When Adam stayed out very late for a few nights, Eve became upset. "You're running around with other women," she charged. "You're being unreasonable," Adam responded. "You're the only woman on earth."

The quarrel continued until Adam fell asleep, only to be awakened by someone poking him in the chest. It was Eve.

"What do you think you're doing?" Adam demanded.

"Counting your ribs," said Eve.

Top Bad Experiences when Renting from U-Haul (G)
1. Tow bar failed. We're still looking for the car.
2. Brakes failed on steep mountain road. When I complained that I was almost killed, they called me a "crybaby".
3. Their "one-way" rental truck couldn't shift into reverse.
4. They insisted that odometer "wrapped around" -- charged me for 1000120 miles.

Deductive Reasoning (PG-13)
A Man approaches to greet a new neighbor who is just moving into the house next door and asks what he does for a living.

Neighbor 1: "I am a professor at the University, I teach deductive reasoning"

Man: "Deductive reasoning, what is that?"

Neighbor 1: "Let me give you and example. I see you have a dog house out back. By that I deduce that you have a dog."

Man: "That is right"

Neighbor 1: "The fact that you have a dog, leads me to deduce that you have a family"

Man: "Right again"

Neighbor 1: "Since you have a family I deduce that you have a wife"

Man: "Correct"

Neighbor 1: "And since you have a wife I can deduce that you are heterosexual."

Man: "Yup"

Neighbor 1: "That is deductive reasoning"

Man: "Cool"

Later that same day...:

Man: "Hey I was talking to that new guy who moved in next door"

Neighbor 2: "Is he a nice guy"

Man: "Yes, and he has an interesting job"
Neighbor 2: "Oh, yeah what does he do "
Man: "He is a professor of deductive reasoning at the University"
Neighbor 2: "Deductive reasoning, what is that?"
Man: "Let me give you an example. Do you have a dog house?"
Neighbor 2: "No"
Man: "Fag."

God Told Him That (G)

Edward Brown, 78, of Dartmouth, Massachusetts, nearly lost his home because he refused to make the final payment of $324.57. Erroneously believing that if he still carried a mortgage, he couldn't be sued for injuries on the property, he simply ignored repeated bills, warnings and an eviction notice until his $90,000 house was seized and sold at auction for $60,000.

The bank finally learned of Brown's mistake, bought his house back for him, and canceled the $324.57 debt. He can use that money to buy insurance! Then somebody tripped on his sidewalk, sued him, and took his house away again.

The Full Mounty (PG-13)

Three entrepreneurs in Houghton, South Africa, have opened a Chippendale's-like club for women called the House of Spartacus, which not only offers strippers, "adult Tupperware parties," and more, but the women can actually have sex with the male dancers for $75 to $175 (U.S.). About 80 percent ask for something unusual rather than just straight sex. One dancer said most are attractive career women who

are unsatisfied at home, and in his whole career as a gigolo, he's only had to sleep with three gross women.
* And he did all three at once, so it was over with quickly.
* He loves his job so much, he'd do it for free!
* Having sex with a male stripper is known as "The Full Mounty."
* For $175, you get to have sex with the dancers who DON'T stuff their G-strings.

POT FARMER WANTS TO MAKE A DEAL (G)

Soldiers in southern Mexico found a marijuana plantation, but the owner seemed to think he could make a deal to save his crop. The pot farm was deserted, but the troops found $11,000 in old dollar bills and a note. It read, "Sirs, with all respect I realize you are just doing your job, but I would like to negotiate. Here are 100,000 pesos, call me on my telephone. Yours sincerely, a friend."
*Now, that's what I call a dealer!
*Those soldiers could never be bought off for $11,000! Not when they could steal the pot and sell it for a million dollars!

The Confessional (R)

Father O'leary is doing confession one Sunday when he realizes he has to pee. He peeks his head out of the confessional and sees a group of altar boys sitting in the pews. He calls out for one and asks the little boy to take his place while he goes to the bathroom, "Whenever they enter, allow them to confess, and using this list, give them the appropriate repentance."

There's a list posted on his side of the confessional. "For theft, 6 hail-Mary's. For murder, 12 hail-Mary's and an hour of silent prayer, and so on, ya got it." The boy nods and proceeds to wait.

Along comes a lady who enters the confessional and begins "Father, it's been 2 weeks since my last confession." The boy, in a low, manly voice responds "Yes, go on my child." She continues to tell him that she gave a blowjob to a man who was not her husband. The boy scans the list saying to himself "Blowjob, blowjob, where's the friggin blowjob". Well there's no listing for blowjob, so he looks out and asks Tony, another altar boy, "Hey Tony, what does Father O'leary give for a blowjob?" Tony goes, "A handful of Gummi Bears and a Snickers bar."

Can I Crash at Your Place (G)

Deadhead Zeke was seeing a show out of town, and was going to crash at his pal Cosmo's place. However, Zeke missed Cosmo after the show, and was feeling pretty lost and disoriented. So he called Cosmo asking how to get to his pad. Cosmo told him to look at a street sign to find out where he was, and he would go pick him up. Zeke looks at the street and says, "I'm at the intersection of Walk, Don't Walk". Cosmo replies "Dude! that's right outside my building!"

Barbie's Letter To Santa: (G)

Dear Santa,
Listen you fat little troll, I've been helping you out every year, playing at being the perfect Christmas Present, wearing skimpy bathing suits in frigid weather, and drowning in fake tea from one too many tea parties, and I hate to break it to ya Santa, but IT'S DEFINITELY PAY BACK TIME! There had better be some changes around here this Christmas, or

I'm gonna call for a nationwide meltdown (and trust me, you won't wanna be around to smell it).

So, here's my holiday wish list for 2000, Santa.

1. Sweat pants and a frumpy, oversized sweatshirt. I'm sick of looking like a hooker. How much smaller are these bathing suits gonna get?

2. Real underwear that can be pulled on and off. Preferably white. What bonehead at Mattel decided to cheap out and MOLD imitation underwear to my skin?!? It looks like cellulite!

3. A REAL man... maybe GI JOE. Hell, I'd take Tickle-Me-Elmo over that wimped-out excuse for a boytoy Ken. And what's with that earring anyway?

4. Breast reduction surgery. I don't care whose arm you have to twist, just get it done.

5. A new, more 90's persona. Maybe "PMS Barbie", complete with a miniature container of chocolate chip cookie dough ice cream and a bag of chips.

6. No more McDonald's endorsements. The grease is wrecking my vinyl.

7. Mattel stock options. It's been 37 years-I think I deserve it.

Okay Santa, that's it. Considering my valuable contribution to society, I don't think these requests are out of line. If you disagree, then you can find yourself a new bitch for next Christmas. It's that simple.

Yours Truly,

Barbie

Ken's Letter To Santa:

Dear Santa,

I understand that one of my colleagues has petitioned you for changes in her contract, specifically asking for anatomical and career changes. In addition, it is my understanding that disparaging remarks were made about me, my ability to please, and some of my fashion choices. I would like to take this opportunity to inform you of some of issues concerning Ms. Barbie, and some of my own needs and desires.

First of all, I along with several other colleagues feel Barbie DOES NOT deserve preferential treatment - the bitch has everything. Along with Joe, Jem, Raggedy Ann & Andy, I DO NOT have a dream house, corvette, evening gowns, and in some cases the ability to change our hair style. I personally have only 3 outfits which I am forced to mix and match at great length. My decision to accessorize my outfits with an earring was my decision and reflects my lifestyle choice. I too would like a change in my career. Have you ever considered "Decorator Ken", "Beauty Salon Ken", or "Out Of Work Actor Ken"? In closing, I would like to point out that any further concessions to the blond bimbo from hell will result in action being taken by myself and others. And Barbie can forget about having Joe he's mine, at least that's what he said last night.
Sincerely,
        Ken

Pigeon Criminals (G)

Authorities investigating the theft of diamonds from South Africa's Alexcor mine said they believed the thieves used carrier pigeons to fly the stolen gems past security checkpoints. South African police shot down a plot to smuggle diamonds via a carrier pigeon -- killing the bird as it rested while transporting the uncut gems.

Residents in Alexander Bay, a diamond-mining region near the Namibian border, noticed the pigeon Wednesday when it landed wearing a band around its chest. Police shot the bird and found six packets of uncut diamonds valued at $11,320.

Quick Wish (PG-13)
Two guys are in a locker room when one guy notices the other guy has a cork in his ass.

He says, "How'd you get a cork in your ass?"

The other guy says, "I was walking along the beach and I tripped over a lamp. There was a puff of smoke, and then a red man in a turban came oozing out. He said, "I am Tonto, Indian Genie. I can grant-um you one wish." And I said, "No shit?"

Farmer's Wife (PG-13)
A man walked up to a farmer's house and knocked on the door. When a woman opened the door, the man ask if she knew how to have sex. Not amused, she slammed the door. Again, the man knocked, and again asked the same question. Again, not amused, she screamed, "Get the hell away!"

Later, she told her husband of the incident. He said he would stay home the following day just in case.

Sure enough, the next day the same man returned. The husband hid with his gun while the lady answered the door. When she was asked again if she knew how to have sex, she said yes.

The man replied, "Great, give some to your husband the next time you see him and tell him to keep away from my wife!!"

THE DIETER'S GUIDE TO (R) WEIGHT LOSS DURING SEX

ACTIVITY	CALORIES BURNED
REMOVING CLOTHES:	
With partner's consent	12
Without partner's consent	187
UNHOOKING BRA:	
Using two calm hands	7
Using one trembling hand	36
ACHIEVING ERECTIONS:	
For normal healthy man	2.5
Losing erection	14
Searching for it	115
PUTTING ON CONDOM:	
With erection	5
Without erection	300
INSERTING DIAPHRAGM:	
If the woman who does it is	
Experienced	6
Inexperienced	73
If a man does it	680
ORGASM:	
Real	27
Faked	
160	

GETTING CAUGHT:
By partner's spouse   60
By your spouse   100
Trying to explain   55
Trying to remain calm   100
Leaping out of bed   75
Getting dressed in one motion   500
Thanking partner quickly   2

The Golfers (PG-13)

Andy and Pete were having an awfully slow round of golf, because the two attractive ladies in front of them managed to get into every sand trap, lake, and rough on the course, and they didn't bother to wave the men on through, which is proper golf etiquette.

After two hours of waiting and waiting, Andy said: "I think I'll walk up there and ask those gals to let us play through."
He walked up the fairway, got halfway to the ladies, stopped, turned around, and came back, explaining: "I can't do it. One of those women is my wife and the other is my mistress. Maybe you'd better go talk to them."

So Pete took off toward the ladies, got halfway there and, just as Andy had done, stopped, turned around, and walked back. In reply to Andy's quizzical look he said only: "Small world."

Question: What does a Dallas Cowboy smell like after sex?
Answer: Pepper Spray!

Modern Logic (G)

Dave Feuerstein sued the British supermarket chain Tesco because one of its promotions offered so many bargains that he hurt his back carrying off the discounted merchandise. "Offers like this are too good to refuse," said Feuerstein, who made several trips to the store over a three-day period to redeem more than 300 coupons. "Tesco should have been more considerate and make it impossible to do what I did. If Tesco hadn't had this offer I wouldn't have hurt my back.

CATCH! [Darwin Award] (G)

A man in Alabama died from rattlesnake bites. Big deal you may say, but there's a twist here that makes him a candidate. It seems he and a friend were playing catch with a rattlesnake. You can guess what happened from here. The friend (a future Darwin Awards candidate) was hospitalized.

A Trick Question (PG-13)

The woman in question, was pulled over for speeding by a California Highway Patrol motorcycle officer. When he walked up to her window and opened his ticket book she said: "I bet you're going to sell me a ticket to the Highway Patrolman's Ball."

He replied, "No, highway patrolmen don't have balls."

There followed a moment of silence while she smiled and he realized what he'd said. He then closed his book, got back on his motorcycle and left.

Double-Take (G)
Dear Mr. _____:
Thank you for your letter of December 1. After careful consideration, I regret to inform you that I am unable to accept your refusal to offer me employment with your firm. This year I have been particularly fortunate in receiving an unusually large number of rejection letters. With such a varied and promising field of candidates, it is impossible for me to accept all refusals.

Despite your company's outstanding qualifications and previous experience in rejecting applicants, I find that your rejection does not meet with my needs at this time. Therefore, I will initiate employment with your firm immediately. I look forward to seeing you. Best of luck in rejecting future candidates.
                                        Sincerely,

What You Are Selling (R)
Two car salesmen were sitting at the bar. One complained to the other, "Boy, business sucks. If I don't sell more cars this month, I'm going to lose my f*cking ass." Too late he noticed a beautiful blonde sitting two stools away.

Immediately, he apologized for his bad language. "That's okay," the blonde replied, "If I don't sell more ass this month, I'm going to lose my f*cking car."

Making Customers (PG-13)
A fellow is going on tour of a factory that produces latex products. At the first stop, he's shown the machine that manufactures baby-bottle nipples. The machine makes a loud Hiss-Pop! noise. "The hiss is the rubber being injected into the mold," explains the guide. "The popping sound is a needle

poking a hole in the end of the nipple."

Later, the tour reaches the part of the factory where condoms are made. The machine makes a noise: Hiss, Hiss, Hiss, Hiss-Pop! "Wait a minute!" says the man taking the tour. "I understand what the hiss is, but what's that pop every so often?" "Oh, it's just the same as in the baby-bottle nipple machine," says the guide. "It pokes a hole in every fourth condom." "Well, that can't be good for the condom!" the man states. The guide replies, "No, but it's great for the baby-bottle nipple business!"

Tricky Questions (G)

Johnny missed his final exam due to the flu, but he'd done so well during the year that the teacher suggested to the principal that they give him an oral exam to make up for the test he'd missed.

The principal agreed so they called Johnny into the office, explained, then the teacher asked, "Johnny what does a cow have four of, that I only have two of?" Johnny replied, "Legs." The teacher asked, "Johnny, what do you have in your pants that I don't have in my pants?"

Johnny replied, "Pockets."

The teacher asked, "Johnny, what is the capital of Italy?" Johnny replied. "Rome."

The teacher turned to the principal and asked, "Should we pass him?"

The principal replied, "Better not ask me, I got the first two wrong!"

Saving Your Job (R)

After attending a party for his boss, the life of the party was nursing a king-size hangover and asked his wife, "What the hell happened?" "As usual, you made an ass of yourself in front of your boss," replied the wife.

"Piss on him," answered the husband. "You did," said the wife, "and he fired you."

"Well, f*ck him," said the husband.

"I did, and you go back to work in the morning."

PING PONG ANYONE? (PG-13)

A 20yr old man came into the ER with a stony mass in his rectum. He said that he and his boyfriend were fooling around with concrete mix, then his boyfriend had the idea of pouring the mix into his ass using a funnel. The concrete then hardened, causing constipation and pain. Under general anesthesia, a perfect concrete cast of the man's rectum was removed, along with a ping pong ball.

The Lawnmower (PG-13)

This preacher was looking for a good used lawnmower one day. He found one at a yard sale that Little Johnny happened to be manning.

"This mower work, son?" the preacher asked. Little Johnny said, "Sure does -- just pull on the cord hard, though."

The preacher took the mower home and when he got ready to mow he yanked and pulled and tugged on that cord. Nothing worked. It wouldn't start. Thinking he'd been swindled, he took the mower back to Little Johnny's house.

"You said this would work if I pulled on the cord hard enough."

"Well," Johnny said, "you need to cuss at it sometimes."

The preacher was aghast. "I've not done that in years!"

"Just keep yanking on that cord, Preacher. It'll come back to you."

Redneck Personal Hygiene (G)

If you have to vacuum the bed, it's time to change the sheets.

Unlike clothes and shoes, a toothbrush should never be a hand-me-down item.

While ears need to be cleaned regularly, this is a job that should be done in private using one's OWN truck keys. Plucking unwanted nose hair is time-consuming work. A cigarette lighter and a small tolerance for pain can accomplish the same goal and save hours.

---

12 Days of Misery (RR)

Dearest John:

I went to the door today and the postman delivered a partridge in a pear tree. What a delightful gift. I couldn't have been more surprised.

With dearest love and affection, Agnes

December 15th

Dearest John:

Today the postman brought your very sweet gift. Just imagine, turtle doves. I'm just delighted at your very thoughtful gift. They are just adorable.

All my love, Agnes

December 16th

Dear John:

Oh, aren't you the extravagant one! Now I must protest. I don't deserve such generosity. Three French hens. They are just darling but I must insist... you're just too kind.

Love Agnes December 17th
Dear John:

Today the postman delivered four calling birds. Now really! They are beautiful, but don't you think enough is enough? You're being too romantic.

Affectionately, Agnes

December 18th

Dearest John:

What a surprise! Today the postman delivered five golden rings. One for each finger. You're just impossible, but I love it. Frankly, John, all those squawking birds were beginning to get on my nerves.

All my love, Agnes

December 19th

Dear John:

When I opened the door there were actually six geese a-laying on my front steps. So you're back to the birds again, huh? Those geese are huge. Where will I ever keep them? The neighbors are complaining and I can't sleep through the racket. Please stop!

Cordially, Agnes

December 20th

John:

What's with you and those f*cking birds???? Seven swans a-swimming. What kind of goddam joke is this? There's bird shit all over the house and they never stop the racket. I'm a nervous wreck and I can't sleep all night. It's not funny! So stop with those f*king birds.

Sincerely, Agnes

December 21st

Ok Buster:

I think I prefer the birds. What the hell am I going to do eight maids a-milking? It's not enough with all those birds and eight maids a-milking, but they had to bring their own goddam cows. There is shit all over the lawn and I can't move into my own house. Just lay off me. Smart ass.

Ag

December 22nd

Hey Shithead:

What are you? Some kind of sadist? Now there's nine pipers playing. And Christ - do they play. They never stopped chasing those maids since they got here yesterday morning. The cows are upset and are stepping all over those screeching birds. No wonder they screech. What am I going to do? The neighbors have started a petition to evict me. You'll get yours.

From Ag

December 23rd

You Rotten Prick:

Now there's ten ladies dancing - I don't know why I call those sluts ladies. They've been balling those nine pipers all night long. Now the cows can't sleep and they've got diarrhea. My living room is a river of shit. The commissioner of buildings has subpoenaed me to give cause why the building shouldn't be condemned. I'm sicking the police on you.

One who means it, Ag

December 24th

Listen F*ckhead:

What's with the eleven lords a-leaping on those maids and afterementioned "ladies?" Some of those broads will never walk again. Those pipers ran through the maids and have been committing sodomy with the cows. All 234 of the birds are dead. They have been trampled to death in the orgy. I hope you're satisfied, you rotten swine.

Your sworn enemy, Miss Agnes McCallister

December 25th (From the law offices Taeker, Spredar, and Baegar)

Dear Sir:

This is to acknowledge your latest gift of twelve fiddlers fiddling, which you have seen fit to inflict on our client, Miss Agnes McCallister. The destruction, of course, was total. All correspondence should come to our attention. If you should attempt to reach Miss McCallister at Happy Dale Sanitarium, the attendants have instructions to shoot you on sight. With this letter, please find attached a warrant for your arrest.

The Jar (PG-13)

A 75-year old man went to his doctor's office to get a sperm count. The doctor gave the man a jar and said, "Take this jar home and bring me back a sample tomorrow."

The next day, the 75-year old man reappears at the doctor's office and gives him the jar, which is as clean and empty as on the previous day. The doctor asks what happened, and the man explains, "Well, doc, it's like this. First I tried with my right hand, but nothing. Then I tried with my left hand, but nothing. Then I asked my wife for help. She tried with her right hand, but nothing. Then her left, but nothing. She even tried with her mouth, first with the teeth in, then with theteeth out, and still nothing.

Hell, we even called up the lady next door, and she tried with both hands and her mouth too, but nothing."

The doctor was shocked. "You asked your NEIGHBOUR?" The old man replied, "Yep, but no matter what we tried, we couldn't get the damn jar open!"

Three Convicts (PG-13)

Three convicts were on the way to prison. They were each allowed to take one item with them to help them occupy their time while incarcerated. On the bus, one turned to another and said, "So, what did you bring?"

The second convict pulled out a box of paints and stated that he intended to paint anything he could. He wanted to become the "Grandma Moses of Jail". Then he asked the first, "What did you bring?"

The first convict pulled out a deck of cards and grinned and said, "I brought cards. I can play poker, solitaire, gin, and any number of games."

The third convict was sitting quietly aside, grinning to himself. The other two took notice and asked, "Why are you so smug? What did you bring?"

The guy pulled out a box of tampons and smiled. He said, "I brought these."

The other two were puzzled and asked, "What can you do with those?"

He grinned and pointed to the box and said, "Well according to the box, I can go horseback riding, swimming, roller-skating...."

"Bathing Like A Woman"
Walk to bathroom wearing long dressing gown and towel on head. If you see your boyfriend/ husband along the way, cover up any exposed flesh immediately, ignore his juvenile turban gags and then rush to bathroom.

Look at your womanly physique in the mirror and stick out your gut so that you can complain and whine even more about how you're getting fat.

Turn on the hot water only.

Get in the shower, once you have found it through all that steam. Look for facecloth, armcloth, legcloth, long loofah, wide loofah and pumice stone.

Wash your hair once with Cucumber and Lamfrey shampoo with 83 added vitamins.

Wash your hair again with Cucumber and Lamfrey shampoo with 83 added vitamins.

Condition your hair with Cucumber and Lamfrey conditioner enhanced with natural crocus oil. Leave on hair for fifteen minutes.

Wash your face with crushed apricot facial scrub for ten miutes until red raw.

Wash entire rest of body with Ginger Nut and Jaffa Cake body wash.

Complain bitterly when you realize that your boyfriend or husband once again been eating your Ginger Nut and Jaffa Cake body wash.

Rinse conditioner off hair (this takes at least fifteen minutes as you must make sure that it has all come off).

Debate shaving armpits and legs and decide that you can't be bothered. Slick hair back and pretend you're like Bo Derek in 10.

Scream loudly when your boyfriend/husband flushes the toilet, and you get a rush of scalding water.

Dry with a towel the size of a small African country.
Check entire body for the remotest sign of a spot.
Check entire head for gray hairs. Attack both with nails/ tweezers if found.
Return to bedroom wearing long dressing gown and towel on head. If you see your boyfriend/ husband along the way, cover up any exposed flesh immediately, ignore his juvenile turban gags and then rush to bedroom.

Heaven Sent (G)

It got crowded in heaven, so, for one day it was decided only to accept people who had really had a bad day on the day they died. St. Peter was standing at the pearly gates and said to the first man, "Tell me about the day you died."

The man said, "Oh, it was awful. I was sure my wife was having an affair, so I came home early to catch her with him. I searched all over the apartment but couldn't find him anywhere. So I went out onto the balcony, we live on the 25th floor, and found this man hanging over the edge by his fingertips. I went inside, got a hammer, and started hitting his hands. He fell, but landed in some bushes. So, I got the refrigerator and pushed it over the balcony and it crushed him. The strain of the act gave me a heart attack, and I died."

St. Peter couldn't deny that this was a pretty bad day, and since it was a crime of passion, he let the man in.

He then asked the next man in line about the day he died.

"Well, sir, it was awful," said the second man. "I was doing aerobics on the balcony of my 26th floor apartment when I twisted my ankle and slipped over the edge. I managed to grab the balcony of the apartment below, but some maniac came out and started pounding on my fingers with a hammer. Luckily I landed in some bushes. But, then the guy dropped a refrigerator on me!"

St. Peter chuckled, let him into heaven and decided he could really start to enjoy this job.

"Tell me about the day you died?", he said to the third man in line. "OK, picture this, I'm naked, hiding inside a refrigerator...."

Where's the Money, Deaf Man? (PG-13)

The Mafia was looking for a new man to make weekly collections from all the private businesses that they were 'protecting'. Feeling the heat from the police force, they decided to use a deaf person for this job--if he were to get caught, he wouldn't be able to communicate to the police what he was doing.

Well, on his first week, the deaf collector picks up over $50,000. He gets greedy, decides to keep the money and stashes it in a safe place. The Mafia soon realizes that their collection is late, and sends some of their hoods after the deaf collector. The hoods find the deaf collector and ask him where the money is. The deaf collector can't communicate with them, so the Mafia drags the guy to an interpreter.

The Mafia hood says to the interpreter, "Ask him where da money is." The interpreter signs, "Where's the money?"

The deaf replies, "I don't know what you're talking about."

The interpreter tells the hood, "He says he doesn't know what you're talking about."

The hood pulls out a .38 pistol and places it in the ear of the deaf collector. "NOW ask him where da money is."

The interpreter signs, "Where is the money?"

The deaf man signs, "The $50,000 is in Central Park, hidden in the third tree stump on the left from the West 78th Street gate."

The interpreter says to the hood, "He says he still doesn't know what you're talking about and doesn't think you have the guts to pull the trigger!"

Real Radio Conversation (G)

This is the actual radio conversation of a US naval ship with Canadian authorities off the coast of Newfoundland in October 1995. Radio conversation released by the chief of naval operations, 10-10-95.

CANADIANS: Please divert your course 15 degrees to the south to avoid a collision.

AMERICANS: Recommend you divert your course 15 degrees to the north to avoid a collision.

CANADIANS: Negative. You will have to divert your course 15 degrees to the south to avoid a collision.

AMERICANS: This is the captain of a US Navy ship. I say again, divert YOUR course.

CANADIANS: No, I say again, you divert YOUR course.
AMERICANS: This is the Aircraft Carrier US LINCOLN, te second largest ship in the United States Atlantic Fleet. We are accompanied with three Destroyers, three Cruisers and numerous support vessels. I DEMAND that you change your course 15 degrees north. I say again, that's one-five degrees north, or counter-measures will be undertaken to ensure the safety of this ship.

CANADIANS: This is a lighthouse. Your call.

Where the Driver is From (G)

One hand on the wheel, one hand on the horn: New York City
One hand on wheel, one finger out window: Chicago
One hand on wheel, one hand cradling cell phone, gun in lap,

brick on accelerator: Los Angeles
Both hands on wheel, eyes shut, both feet on brake, quivering in terror: Ohio, but driving in California.
Both hands in air, gesturing, both feet on accelerator, head turned to talk to someone in back seat: Italy
One hand on wheel, one hand hanging out the window, keeping speed steadily at 70mph, driving down the center of the road unless coming around a blind curve, in which case they are on the left side of the road: male from rural Texas

Four wheel drive pickup truck, shotgun mounted in rear window, beer cans on floor, squirrel tails attached to antenna: West Virginia male.

Two hands gripping wheel, blue hair barely visible above window level, driving 35 on the interstate in the left lane with the left blinker on: Florida

---

Welcome to the Church (PG-13)

Three couples, an elderly couple, a middle-aged couple and a young newlywed couple wanted to join a church. The pastor said, "We have special requirements for new parishioners. You must abstain from having sex for two weeks." The couples agreed and came back at the end of two weeks.

The pastor went to the elderly couple and asked, "Were you able to abstain from sex for the two weeks?" The old man replied, "No problem at all, Pastor." "Congratulations! Welcome to the church!" said the pastor.

The pastor went to the middle-aged couple and asked, "Well, were you able to abstain from sex for the two weeks?" The man replied, "The first week was not too bad. The second week I had to sleep on the couch for a couple of nights but, yes we made it." "Congratulations! Welcome to the church!" said the pastor.

The pastor then went to the newlywed couple and asked, "Well, were you able to abstain from sex for two weeks?" "No Pastor, we were not able to go without sex for the two weeks,"the young man replied sadly. "What Happened?" inquired the pastor.

"My wife was reaching for a can of corn on the top shelf and dropped it. When she bent over to pick it up, I was overcome with lust and took advantage of her right there."

"You understand, of course, this means you will not be welcome in our church," stated the pastor.

"We know." said the young man, "We're not welcome at Safeway anymore either."

Drug-Abuse by Cartoon Characters (PG-13)
Olive Oyl

Probably Dexatrim abuse, maybe some amphetamines. Who is that skinny?! She might even be anorexic, she is always giving her burger to her friend. One side question, what the hell are Popeye and Brutus thinking? What is it, her personality?

Droopy

The number one downer abuser in toon land. Can't someone slip him an upper every year or two. The only time I ever saw him happy is when he sees the picture of the babe. Sort of makes you wonder.

He-Man

This is an easy one. I mean c'mon. Roid monkey #1. "BY THE POWER OF ANABOL!!!!!!" Makes me want to root for Skeletor. Alone in his castle, hitting the weights.

Daffy Duck

If he isn't using crack, Marion Barry is clean. He is so wired he bounces around on his head without pain. Blows his beak off all the time. Some symptoms might be from "daffiness" but Haldol wouldn't work for him.

Dopey Dwarf

He openly admits it. The other dwarfs deny involvement but they are under investigation. Allegations are that Doc is writing some extra scripts for Sneezy and all the guys partaking are afloat.

Doctor Saves the Day (R)

A husband and wife are on a nudist beach when suddenly a wasp buzzes into the wife's rear end. Naturally enough, she panics. The husband is also quite shaken but manages to pull a coat over her, pull up his shorts, and rush to the car.

Then, the husband makes a mad dash to the doctor. The doctor, after examining her, says that the wasp is in too far to remove it with forceps. The doctor suggests putting honey on the husband's penis. The plan is to entice the wasp and to withdrawal as soon as he feels the wasp.

At this point, the husband and wife agree, they'll do anything to get the wasp out. And so, the honey is smeared on the husband's penis. Because of his wife's screaming and the panic in the room, the husband is unable to rise to the occasion. The doctor offers to perform the deed as long as the couple don't object. Naturally, both agree, for fear the wasp will do serious damage.

The doctor quickly undresses, smears the honey on his penis, and instantly gets an erection. He proceeds to entice the wasp, and does so with vigor. The doctor, almost breathless, appears to be reaching orgasm. The husband shouts, "What the hell's happening?" Replies the doctor, "Change of plan. I"m going to drown the bastard!"

Real Courage (G)
A student taking a philosophy class had a single question on his final: "What is courage?".

The student wrote "This.", signed it, and turned it in.

Take That (G)
One professor at school (an econ prof) had a strict policy that the hourly examinations were done at the bell and anyone who kept writing on their exam after the bell would take a zero on the exam. Well, one guy kept writing on his exam for a while after the bell and then confidently strode up to turn it in. The prof looked at him and said "Don't bother to hand that paper in...you get a zero for continuing after the bell."

The guy looked at him and said, "Professor, do you know who I am!!" The professor replied, "No, and I don't care if your dad is president of the United States...you get a zero on this exam"

The guy, with a enraged look on his face, shouted, "You mean you have no idea who I am???"

The professor responded, "No, I've no idea who you think you are." With that, the guy said "good," plunged his exam into the middle of the stack of other students exams, and did a hasty retreat from the examination room!!!

Nevermind (G)
When an armed robber who took less than $100 from a 7-11 store in St. Peters, MO, couldn't get his get-away car started, he returned to the store, handed back the money and told the two clerks it was all just a joke. They agreed to give his vehicle a jump start, not to write down his license plate number and wait about 40 minutes before calling the police.

"We have a friendly town out here," police Officer David Kuppler noted, indicating the suspect was arrested anyway about an hour later.

Not the Same Old School Excuses (G)
LEESVILLE, La. - "My son is under the doctor's care and should not take PE today," one parent wrote. "Please execute him."

Another had a more comprehensive request: "Please excuse Fred for being. It was his father's fault."
"Please excuse Jay being absent on Jan. 28, 29, 30, 31, 32 and 33," wrote a parent who lives by an unusual calendar.

And in an extreme case of people losing things, "Please excuse Carl from PE for a few days. He fell yesterday out of a tree and misplaced his hip."

"Please excuse Justin for being absent. He had a cold and could not breed well."

Yechh (PG-13)
A teacher was working with a group of children, trying to broaden their horizons through sensory perception. She brought in a variety of lifesavers and said, "Children, I'd like

you to close your eyes and taste these."

The kids easily identified the taste of cherries, lemons and mint, but when the teacher gave them honey-flavored lifesavers, all of the kids were stumped.

"I'll give you a hint," said the teacher. "It's something your daddy and mommy probably call each other all the time."
Instantly, one of the kids coughed his onto the floor and shouted, "Spit 'em out, guys, they're as*holes!"

Darwin Award Candidate (G)

To poacher, Marino M. of Spain, who shot a stag standing above him on an overhanging rock-and was killed instantly when it fell on him.

Bad Day at the Office (G)

Hi Sis, Just another note from your bottom dwelling brother. Last week I had a bad day at the office. Before I can tell you what happened to me, I first must bore you with a few technicalities of my job. As you know my office lies at the bottom of the sea. I wear a suit to the office. It's a wetsuit. This time of year the water is quite cool. So what we do to keep warm is this: We have a diesel powered industrial water heater. This $20,000 piece of crap sucks the water out of the sea. It heats it to a delightful temp. It then pumps it down to the diver through a garden hose which is taped to the air hose.

Now this sounds like a damn good plan, and I've used it several times with no complaints. What I do, when I get to the bottom and start working, is I take the hose and stuff it down the back of my neck. This floods my whole suit with warm water. It's like working in a jacuzzi.

Everything was going well until all of a sudden, my butt

started to itch. So, of course, I scratched it. This only made things worse. Within a few seconds my butt started to burn. I pulled the hose out from my back, but the damage was done. In agony I realized what had happened. The hot water machine had sucked up a jellyfish and pumped it into my suit.

This is even worse than the poison ivy you once had under your cast. Now I had that hose down my back. I don't have any hair on my back, so the jellyfish couldn't get stuck to my back. My butt crack was not as fortunate. When I scratched what I thought was an itch, I was actually grinding the jellyfish into my butt. I informed the dive supervisor of my dilemma over the comms. His instructions were unclear due to the fact that he, along with 5 other divers were laughing hysterically. Needless to say I aborted the dive. I was instructed to make 3 agonizing in-water decompression stops totaling 35 minutes before I could come to the surface for my chamber dry decompression.

I got to the surface wearing nothing but my helmet. My suit and gear were tied to the bell. When I got on board, the medic, with tears of laughter running down his face, handed me a tube of cream and told me to shove it up my butt when I get in the chamber. The cream put the fire out, but I couldn't crap for two days because my butt was swollen shut. I later found out that this could easily have been prevented if the suction hose was placed on the leeward side of the ship.

Anyway, the next time you have a bad day at the office, think of me. Think about how much worse your day would be if you were to shove a jellyfish up your butt. I hope you have no more bad days at the office. But, if you do, I hope this will make it more tolerable.

    Your Brother,
        Brian

Real Embarrassing Radio (PG-13)
On the morning show at a radio station in Chicago they play a game for prizes usually vacations and such, called "Mate Match." The DJ's ring someone at work and ask if they are married or in a serious relationship.

If yes, then this person is asked 3 very personal questions that vary from couple to couple and asked for their significant others name and work phone number. If the significant other answers correctly then they are winners.

This particular day it got interesting:

DJ: HEY! This is Edgar on WBAM. Do you know "Mate Match"?
Contestant:(laughing) Yes I do.
DJ: What is your name? First only please.
Contestant: Brian
DJ: Are you married or what Brian?
Brian: Yes.
DJ: Thank you Brian. OK, now, what is your wife's name? First only please Brian.
Brian: Sara.
DJ: Is Sara at work Brian?
Brian: She is gonna kill me.
DJ: Stay with me here Brian! Is she at work?
Brian:(laughing) Yes she is.
DJ: All right then, first question: When was the last time you had sex?
Brian: She is gonna kill me.
DJ: BRIAN! Stay with me here man.
Brian: About 8 o'clock this morning.
DJ: Atta boy.
Brian:(laughing sheepishly) Well.
DJ: Number 2: How long did it last?
Brian: About 10 minutes.
DJ: Wow! You really want that trip huh? No one would ever have said that if there weren't a trip at stake.
Brian: Yeah, it would be really nice.
DJ: OK. Final question: Where was it that you had sex at 8

this morning?
Brian: (laughing hard) I ummmmm...
DJ: This sounds good Brian where was it?
Brian: Not that it was all that great just that her mom is staying with us for a couple of weeks and she was taking a shower at the time.
DJ: Ooooooh, sneaky boy!
Brian: On the kitchen table.
DJ: "Not that great"? That is more adventurous than the last hundred times I have done it. Anyway, (to audience) I will put Brian on hold, get his wife's work number and call her up. You listen to this.
DJ: (to audience) Let's call Sara shall we? (touch tones *ringing*)
DJ: Hey, is Sara around there somewhere?
Clerk: This is she.
DJ: Sara, this is Edgar with WBAM. I have been speaking with Brian for a couple of hours now
Sara: (laughing) A couple of hours?
DJ: Well, a while anyway. He is also on the line with us. Brian knows not to give away any answers or you lose. Soooooooo, do you know the rules of "Mate Match"?
Sara: Yes
DJ: Good.
Sara: (laughing) Brian, what the hell are you up to?
Brian: (laughing) Just answer his questions honestly OK?
Sara: Oh, Brian
DJ: Yeah, yeah, yeah. Sara I will now ask you 3 questions and if you answer what Brian has said then the 2 of you are off to Orlando Florida at our expense. This does include tickets to Disney World, Sea World and tickets to see the Orlando Magic play. Get it Sara?
Sara: (laughing hard) YES, yes.
DJ: All right, when did you have sex last Sara?
Sara: Oh God, Brian...this morning before Brian went to work.
DJ: What time?

Sara: About 8 I think. (sound effect) DING DING DING
DJ: Very good. Next question: How long did it last?
Sara: 12,15 minutes maybe.
DJ: hhmmmmm
Background voice in studio: That's close enough. I am sure she is trying not to harm his manhood.
DJ: Well, we will give you that one. Last question: Where did you do it?
Sara: OH MY GOD, BRIAN! You did not tell them did you?!?!
Brian: Just tell him honey.
DJ: What is bothering you so much Sara?
Sara: Well, It's just that my mom is vacationing with us and...
DJ: SHE SAW?!?!
Sara: Dear Lord,..I cannot believe you told them this.
Brian: Come on honey it's for a trip to Florida.
DJ: Let's go Sara we ain't got all day. Where did you do it?
Sara: In the ass.
DJ: We will be right back.
DJ: I am sorry for that ladies and gentlemen. This is live radio and these things do happen. Anyway, Brian and Sara are off to lovely Orlando, Florida.

Nerd Strikes Back (PG-13)

A very shy guy goes into a bar and sees a beautiful woman sitting at the bar. After an hour of gathering up his courage he finally goes over to her and asks, tentatively, "Um, would you mind if I chatted with you for a while?"

She responds by yelling, at the top of her lungs, "No, I won't sleep with you tonight!" Everyone in the bar is now staring at them.

Naturally, the guy is hopelessly and completely embarrassed and he slinks back to his table.

After a few minutes, the woman walks over to him and

apologizes. She smiles at him and says, "I'm sorry if I embarrassed you. You see, I'm a graduate student in psychology and I'm studying how people respond to embarrassing situations."

To which he responds, at the top of his lungs, "What do you mean $200?"

The Power of Exposure (PG-13)

AUGUSTA, ME - Four people were injured in a string of bizarre accidents. Sherry M. was admitted with a head wound caused by flying masonry, Tim V. was diagnosed with a mild case of whiplash and contusions on his chest, arms, and face, Bryan C. suffered torn gum tissue, and Pamela K. first two fingers of her right hand had been bitten off.

Sherry had just dropped her husband off for his first day of work and, in addition to a good-bye kiss, she flashed her breasts at him. "I'm still not sure why I did it," she said later. "I was really close to the car, so I didn't think anyone would see. Besides, it couldn't have been for more than two seconds." However, cab driver Tim did see and lost control of his cab, running over the curb and into the corner of the Johnson Medical Building. Inside, Pamela, a dental technician, was cleaning Bryan's teeth. The crash of the cab against the building made Pamela jump, tearing Bryan's gums with the cleaning pick. In shock, he bit down, severing two fingers from Pamela's hand. Sherry's wound was caused by a falling piece of medical building.

God Was Watching (PG-13)

TACOMA, WA - Kerry Bingham had been drinking with several friends when one of them said they knew a person who had bungee-jumped from the Tacoma Narrows Bridge in the middle of traffic. The conversation grew more heated and at least 10 men trooped along the walkway of the bridge at 4:30 a.m. Upon arrival at the midpoint of the bridge they discovered that no one had brought bungee rope. Bingham, who had continued drinking, volunteered and pointed out that a coil of lineman's cable lay nearby. One end of the cable was secured around Bingham's leg and the other end was tied to the bridge. His fall lasted 40 feet before the cable tightened and tore his foot off at the ankle. He miraculously survived his fall into the icy river water and was rescued by two nearby fishermen. "All I can say," said Bingham,"is that God was watching out for me on that night. There's just no other explanation for it." Bingham's foot was never located.

Creative Response to IRS (G)

There was a man who computed his taxes for 1999 and found that he owed $3407. He packaged up his payment and included this letter:

Dear IRS:

Enclosed is my 1999 Tax Return & payment. Please take note of the attached article from the USA Today newspaper. In the article, you will see that the Pentagon is paying $171.50 for hammers and NASA has paid $600.00 for a toilet seat.

Please find enclosed four toilet seats (value $2400) and six hammers (value $1029).

This brings my total payment to $3429.00. Please note the overpayment of $22.00 and apply it to the 'Presidential Election Fund', as noted on my return. Might I suggest you the send the above mentioned fund a '1.5 inch screw'. (See attached article - HUD paid $22.00 for a 1.5 inch Phillips Head Screw.)

It has been a pleasure to pay my tax bill this year, and I look forward to paying it again next year. I just saw an article about the Pentagon and 'screwdrivers'.
     Sincerely,

     I. Getscrewed Everyear

Falkland Islands (PG-13)

A British General had sent some of his men off to fight for their country in the Falkland Island Crisis.
Upon returning to England from the South American island, three soldiers that had distinguished themselves in battle were summoned to the General's office.

"Since we weren't actually at war," the General began, "I can't give out any medals. We did, however, want to let each of you know your efforts were appreciated."

"What we've decided to do is to let each of you choose two points on your body. You will be given 2 pounds sterling for each inch of distance between those parts. We'll start on the left, boys, so what'll it be?"

Soldier 1: "The tip of me head to me toes, sahr!"
General: "Very good son, that's 70 inches which comes to 140 pounds"

Soldier 2: "The tip of the finger on one outstretched hand to the tip of the other, sir!"
General: "Even better son, that's 72 inches which comes to 144 pounds"

Soldier 3: "The tip of me dick to me balls, sahr!"
General: "That's a strange request, but drop your trousers, son!

As the general begins the measurement: "My god, son, where are your balls?"

Soldier 3: "Falkland Island, sahr!"

What Happened to Good Old Fashion Values (G)
After a bank robber in Metz, France, was let out of jail due to a clerical error, he asked police to return $100,000 he stole during several bank raids. "I simply want them to return money which was honestly stolen," said Phillipe Thomas, "It's a scandal to have your savings stolen."

Daddy is Safe (PG-13)
One night a father overheard his son saying his prayers "God bless Mommy and Daddy and Grammy. Goodbye Grampa."

Well, the father thought it was strange, but he soon forgot about it. The next day, the Grandfather died. About a month or two later the father heard his son saying his prayers again "God bless Mommy. God bless Daddy. Goodbye Grammy."

The next day the grandmother died. Well, the father was getting more than a little worried about the whole situation. Two weeks later, the father once again overheard his sons prayers. "God Bless Mommy. Good bye Daddy."

This alone nearly gave the father a heart attack. He didn't say anything but he got up early to go to work, so that he would miss the traffic. He stayed all through lunch and dinner. Finally after midnight he went home. He was still alive! When he got home he apologized to his wife. "I am sorry Honey. I had a very bad day at work today."

"You think you've had a bad day? YOU THINK YOU'VE HAD A BAD DAY!?" the wife yelled, "The mailman dropped dead on my doorstep this morning!"

A Good Nights Sleep (PG-13)
By the time the sailor pulled into a little town, every hotel

room was taken.

"You've got to have a room somewhere" he pleaded, "or just a bed, I don't care where."

"Well, I do have a double room with one occupant - an Air Force guy," admitted the manager, "and he might be glad to split the cost. But to tell you the truth, he snores so loudly that people in adjoining rooms have complained in the past. I'm not sure it'd be worth it to you."

"No problem," the tired Navy man assured him, "I'll take it."

The next morning the sailor came down to breakfast bright-eyed and bushy-tailed. "How'd you sleep?" asked the manager.

"Never better."

The manager was impressed. "No problem with the other guy snoring?"

"Nope, I shut him up in no time," said the Navy guy.

"How'd you manage that?" asked the manager.

"He was already in bed, snoring away, when I came in the room," the sailor explained.

"I went over, gave him a kiss on the cheek, and said,

"Goodnight, beautiful," and he sat up all night watching me."

Who's The Guy In The Picture (R)

While enjoying a drink with a friend one night, this guy decides to try his luck with an attractive young girl sitting alone by the bar. To his surprise, she asks him to join her for a drink and eventually asks him if he'd like to come back to her place.

The pair jump into a taxi and as soon as they get back to her house, they dive onto the bed and spend the night hard at it. She gives this fellow the best night of his life with great bj's, .. THE WORKS!

Finally, the fellow is completely worn out, and he reaches for a cigarette from his jeans and searches for his lighter.

Unable to find it, he asks the girl if she has one.

"There might be some matches in the top drawer," she replies.

Opening the drawer of the bedside table, he finds a box of matches sitting neatly on top of a framed picture of another man. Naturally, the guy begins to worry. "Is this your husband?" he inquires nervously.

"No, silly," she replies, snuggling up to him.

"Your boyfriend then?"

"No, I don't have a boyfriend," she says, nibbling away at his ear.

"Well, who is he then?!" demands the bewildered guy.

She tells him, "That was me before the operation!"

The Test (G)

A driver was pulled over by a police officer for speeding. As the officer was writing the ticket, he noticed several machetes in the car. "What are those for?" he asked suspiciously. "I'm a juggler," the man replied. "I use those in my act." "Well show me," the officer demanded.

So he got out the machetes and started juggling them, first three, then more, finally seven at one time, overhand, underhand, behind the back, putting on a dazzling show and amazing the officer. Another car passed by. The driver did a double take, and said, "My God, I've got to give up the drink! Look at the test they're giving now!"

Children's Questions (G)

Dear God,
Did you mean for the giraffe to look like that or was it an accident?
                    Norma

Dear God,
Instead of letting people die and having to make new ones, why don't you just keep the ones you have now?
                    Jane

Dear God,
Who draws the lines around the countries?
                    Nan

Dear God,
Thank you for my baby brother, but what I prayed for was a puppy.
                    Joyce

Dear God,
Please send me a pony. I never asked for anything before. You can look it up.
                    Bruce

Dear God,
My brothers told me about being born, but it doesn't sound

right. They are just kidding, aren't they?
                    Marsha

Dear God,
We read that Thomas Edison made light. But in Sunday school, we learned that you did it. So I bet he stole your idea.
                    Sincerely,
                    Donna

Dear God,
I do not think anybody could be a better God. Well, I just want you to know that I am not just saying this because you are God already.
                    Charles

Dear God,
Maybe Cain and Abel would not kill each other so much if they had their own rooms. It works with my brother.
                    Larry

Sexist Men Comments (PG-13)
How are husbands like lawn mowers? They're hard to get started, they emit noxious odors, and half the time they don't work.

How do men define a "50/50" relationship?
We cook-they eat; we clean-they dirty; we iron-they wrinkle.

How do men exercise on the beach?
By sucking in their stomachs every time they see a bikini.

How does a man show he's planning for the future?
He buys two cases of beer instead of one.

How many men does it take to screw in a light bulb?
One-He just holds it up there and waits for the world to revolve around him.

What's a man's idea of honesty in a relationship?
Telling you his real name.

Why did God create man before woman?
He didn't want any advice.
Why do men name their penises?
Because they don't like the idea of having a stranger make 90% of their decisions.

Why do men need instant replay on TV sports?
Because after 30 seconds they forget what happened.

Why does it take 100 million sperms to fertilize one egg?
Because not one will stop and ask for directions.

Why is it difficult to find men who are sensitive, caring and good looking?
They all already have boyfriends.

A Nineties Kind Of Situation(R)
A nun gets into a cab in New York. She demurely says in a small, high voice, "Could you please take me to Times Square?" In a thick Brooklyn accent the cabby initiates conversation, "He sista, that's kinda a long drive? You mind if we, like, chat?"

"Why no, my son, whatever is on your mind?"

"About this celibacy thing. Are you telling me you never think about doin'it?"

"Why certainly, my son, the thought has crossed my mind a time or two. I am of weak human flesh, you understand!"

"Well would ya ever consider, you know doin'it?"

The nun thinks a while

"Well, I suppose under certain conditions, in a very unique circumstance, I might consider it."

"Well, what would dose conditions happen to be?"

"He'd have to be Catholic, unmarried and, well certainly he could have no children."

"Sista, today is your lucky day. I'm all three. Why do youse come on up here... I won't even make you really break your vows. All you gotta do is go down on me."

The nun looks around... They are awfully far away from where anyone would recognize her...at the next light she gets into the front with the driver. By the next light, the nun is getting back into the rear of the cab, and the cabby is smiling from ear to ear. As she settles in, the nun hears the cabby begin to laugh. She inquires,

"Why, my son, what is so humorous?"

The cabby sneers, "Sista, I got ya. I'm Protestand, I'm married, and I got four kids."

And from the back of the cab comes the nun's low voiced response, "Yeah, well, my name's Dave and I'm on my way to a costume party."

Redneck Entertaining in Your Home (G)
A centerpiece for the table should never be anything prepared by a taxidermist.

Do not allow the dog to eat at the table, no matter how good his manners are.

If your dog falls in love with a guest's leg, have the decency to leave them alone for a few minutes.

Fake Death Expert (G)

A man was sentenced last week to two years in prison for faking his death three times to beat drunk driving charges. Peter C. Gentry was first arrested in 1991, but an official looking death certificate sent to authorities said he had died in a Los Angeles auto crash, and the case was dismissed. In 1994, he was arrested again and sent in another death certificate. A year later, Gentry was again arrested and supposedly died this time of "denzor hemorrhagic fever" in Africa. There is no such disease.

Darwin Award Candidate (G)

Mr. Puelo, 32, was apparently being disorderly in a St. Louis market. When the clerk threatened to call police, Puelo grabbed a hot dog, shoved it in his mouth, and walked out without paying for it.

Police found him unconscious in front of the store: paramedics removed the six-inch wiener from his throat, where it had choked him to death.

Potential and Reality (PG-13)

Johnny comes home from school with a writing assignment to define and subsequently explain the difference between potential and reality. After getting nowhere on it for 2 hours, he finally asks his father for help.

"Dad, can you tell me the difference between potential and

reality?" His father looks up, thoughtfully, and then says, "Go ask your mother if she would sleep with Robert Redford for a million dollars. Then go ask your sister, Suzie, if she would sleep with Brad Pitt for a million dollars. Then come back and tell me what they said." The kid is puzzled, but he decides to follow his father's guidance. He goes downstairs to the kitchen and asks his mother, "Mom, if Robert Redford gave you a million dollars to sleep with him would you?" His mother looks around slyly, and then with a little smile on her face says, "Yes, I would." Then he goes back upstairs to his sisters room and asks her, "Sis, if Brad Pitt gave you a million dollars, to sleep with him would you?" His sister looks up and says, "Omigod! Definitely!"

The kid goes back to his room and father and says, "Dad, they both said 'Yes.' " The father sits back and says "Now son potentially, we are sitting on two million bucks, but in reality, we are living with a couple of whores."

The Parrot and the Burglar(G)

Late one night, a burglar broke into a house he thought was empty. He tiptoed through the living room but suddenly he froze in his tracks when he heard a loud voice say: "Jesus is watching you!"

Silence returned to the house, so the burglar crept forward again. "Jesus is watching you," the voice boomed again. The burglar stopped dead again. He was frightened. Frantically, he looked all around. In a dark corner, he spotted a bird cage and in the cage was a parrot. He asked the parrot: "Was that you who said Jesus is watching me?"

"Yes", said the parrot.

The burglar breathed a sigh of relief, and asked the parrot: "What's your name?"

"Clarence," said the bird.

"That's a dumb name for a parrot," sneered the burglar.

"What idiot named you Clarence?"

The parrot said, "The same idiot who named the Rottweiller Jesus."

The Taboo Subject (G)

A minister gave a talk to the Lion's Club on sex. When he got home he couldn't tell his wife that he had spoken on sex, so he said he had discussed horseback riding with the members. A few days later, she ran into some men at the shopping center and they complimented her on the speech her husband had made. She said, "Yes, I heard. I was surprised about the subject matter, as he's only tried it twice. The first time he got so sore he could hardly walk, and the second time he fell off."

Bad Day (PG-13)

Early One Morning A young Jewish couple had only recently set up housekeeping when an unfortunate incident occurred. Early one morning, the wife, drowsy from bed, went to the toilet for the morning's relief, and neglected to notice that the seat was up. When she sat, she kept going! She was just the right size and shape so that she became jammed into the toilet past her waist with her legs sticking straight up in front of her. She cried for her husband, who rushed in, and for the next hour tried desperately to extricate her. In this process they removed her sleeping gown, but this only left her naked and still stuck, with a particular part of her anatomy prominently visible between her splayed legs.

Finally, the couple resolved to call a plumber, despite the embarrassing nature of their problem. When the plumber arrived, the young man let him in, but as they were walking to the bathroom, the young man realized that his wife was exposed in a very compromising and humiliating way. Thinking fast, he ran ahead of the plumber and placed the first thing he could think of, his yamulka skull cap, over his wife's exposed privates. The plumber walked into the bathroom, took one long look, and commented: "Well, I think I can save your wife, buddy, but the Rabbi's a goner."

Reverse Psychology (PG-13)
A man's wife asks him to go to the store to buy some cigarettes. The husband walks down to the store only to find it closed and so he goes into a nearby bar to use the vending machine. At the bar he sees a beautiful woman and starts talking to her. They have a couple of drinks and one thing leads to another. Sometime thereafter, they end up back at the woman's apartment.

One thing leads to another and the next thing the man knows, it's 3 o'clock in the morning. "Oh no!" says the man, "It's really late... my wife's going to kill me. Hey, do you have any talcum powder?" Curious, the woman reluctantly hands the man some talcum powder. He proceeds to rub the powder on his hands and then rushes out the woman's apartment for home.

His wife is waiting for him in the doorway and she is rather upset, to say the least. "Where the hell have you been?"

"Well, honey, its like this. I went to the store like you asked, but they were closed. So, I went to the bar to use the vending machine. Well, I met this great looking girl there and we had a few drinks together. Anyway, one thing led to another and I ended back at her place."

"Oh, really?" says the wife, sarcastically. "Let me see your hands!"

He raises his hands and, sure enough, she notices that his hands are covered with powder. "You son of a bitch! You went bowling again!

Darwin Award Candidate (G)

A San Anselmo, California man died yesterday when he hit a lift tower at the Mammoth Mountain ski area while riding down the slope on a foam pad, authorities said. Matthew H., 22, was pronounced dead at Centinela Mammoth Hospital. The accident occurred about 3 a.m., the Mono County Sheriff's Department said. Matthew and his friends apparently had hiked up a ski run called Stump Alley and undid some yellow foam protectors from the lift towers, said Lieutenant Mike D. of the Mammoth Lakes Police Department. The pads are used to protect skiers who might hit the towers. The group apparently used the pads to slide down the ski slope and Matthew crashed into a tower. It has since been investigated that the tower he hit was the one with its pad removed.

The Secretary (PG-13)

A businessman and his secretary are overcome by passion, and the exec convinces his paramour to retire to his house for what is popularly termed a "nooner."

"Don't worry," he purrs. "My wife is out of town on a business trip, and won't bother us." The pair are necking in the business man's bedroom, when the secretary gasps, "We got to stop now! I'm not using any birth control..."

"No problem," he replies. "I know where my wife keeps her diaphragm." He immediately begins rooting around in the bathroom. After a half hour, he returns to the bedroom in a fury. "That woman!" he exclaims. "She took it with her! I always knew she didn't trust me ....."

No 'Baby Tal' In The First Grade (PG-13)

A new group of first graders were in class for the first time.

The teacher told them, "You are in first grade now and we do not talk 'babytalk' in my classroom. When I point to you, stand, tell me your name, and something you did this summer."

The first child stood, "My name is Jackie, I visited my Nanny." The teacher said "That's great, but from now on we will say grandmother. There is no 'baby talk' in the first grade."

The second child stood, "My name is Regina. I rode a choo choo this summer." The teacher replied, "That's good, but from now on we will say train. Remember, no 'baby talk' in first grade."

The third child stood, "My name is Frank and I read a book this summer." The teacher replied, "That's wonderful Frank! What book did you read?"

The little boy very proudly replied, "Winnie the Shit."

Clara Claus Sues for Divorce (PG-13)

NORTH POLE (UPI) - The unthinkable has happened to ring in the new year: Clara Claus has thrown the jolly fat one out of their home and filed for a divorce.

This court action could put an end to Christmas as we know it.

Mrs. Claus told this reporter, "First it was the reindeer. He claimed he was doing experiments in animal husbandry. Then the elves all started acting skittish whenever he was around. Now he's hanging around with that young girl, Christmas Carol. She's always wearing that short fir-trimmed skirt and that red bodysuit. I know it's cold up here, but do they have to be so perky and pointy all the time? He said he'd be out of town for a day delivering presents. I caught him [expletive deleted] that [expletive deleted] in the toy factory, while the elves made his yearly rounds for him. My lawyer said half of everything is mine. Let's see him make the trip next year with 4 reindeer hauling his fat ass around in a little red wagon.

San Francisco (G)

Two boys are playing football in Golden Gate Park when one is attacked by a Rottweiler. Thinking quickly, the other boy rips off a board of the nearby fence, wedges it down the dog's collar and twists, breaking the dog's neck.

A reporter who is strollin by sees the incident, and rushes over to interview the boy. "Forty Niners' fan saves friend from vicious animal", he starts writing in his notebook.

"But I'm not a Niners fan," the boy replies.

"Oakland Raiders' fan rescues friend from horrific attack," the reporter starts again.

"I'm not a Raiders fan either," the boy says. "Then what are you?" the reporter says.

"I'm a Cowboys fan!!!"

The reporter starts a new sheet in his notebook and writes, "Redneck bastard kills family pet".

Heartbreak, Then Revenge (PG-13)

Two high school sweethearts who went out together for four years inhigh school were both virgins; they enjoyed losing their virginity with each other in 10th grade. When they graduated, they wanted to both go to the same college but the girl was accepted to a college onthe east coast, and the guy went to the west coast. They agreed to be faithful to each other and spend anytime they could together.

As time went on, the guy would call the girl and she would never be home, and when he wrote, she would take weeks to return the letters. Even when he emailed her, she took days to return his messages.

Finally, she confessed to him she wanted to date around. He didn't take this very well and increased his calls, letters, and emails trying to win back her love. Because she became annoyed, and now had a new boyfriend, she wanted to get him off her back.

So, what she did is this: she took a Polaroid picture of her sucking her new boyfriend's unmentionables and sent it to her old boyfriend with a note reading, "I found a new boyfriend, leave me alone."

Well, needless to say, this guy was heartbroken but, even more so, was pissed. So, what he did next was awesome.

He wrote on the back of the photo the following, "Dear Mom and Dad, having a great time at college, please send more money!" and mailed the picture to her parents.

The Prudish Receptionist (R)

A man walked into a crowded doctor's office. As he approached the desk, the receptionist asked "Yes, Sir. May we help you?"

"There's something wrong with my dick," he replied.

The receptionist became aggravated and said, "You shouldn't come into a crowded office and say things like that."

"Why not? You asked me what was wrong and I told you." he said.

"We do not use language like that here," she said. "Please go outside and come back in and say that there's something wrong with your ear or whatever."

The man walked out, waited several minutes and re-entered. The receptionist smiled smugly and asked, "Yes?"

"There's something wrong with my ear," he stated. The receptionist nodded approvingly. "And what is wrong with your ear, Sir?"

"I can't piss out of it." the man replied.

12 Important Rules Of Combat (G)

1. If the enemy is in range, so are you.

2. Don't look conspicuous: it draws fire.
3. Try to look unimportant, they may be low on ammo.
4. Teamwork is essential; it gives the enemy someone else to shoot at.
5. If your attack is going well, you have walked into an ambush.
6. Don't draw fire, it irritates the people around you.
7. The only thing more accurate than incoming enemy fire is incoming friendly fire.
8. When the pin is pulled, Mr. Grenade is not our friend.
9. When in doubt empty the magazine.
10. Never share a fox hole with anyone braver than you.
11. Five second fuses only last three seconds.
12. It is generally inadvisable to eject directly over the area you just bombed.

Doctor's Affair With His Nurse

A doctor started having an affair with his nurse, and shortly after this started, she announced that she had become pregnant.

Not wanting his wife to find out, he gave her a large amount of money and asked her to go out of the country, to Germany, to wait out the pregnancy and have the baby over there.

"But, how will you know when our baby is born?" she asked.

"Well," he said, "After you've had the baby, just send me a post card and write 'sauerkraut' on the back."

Not knowing what else to do, she took the money and went off to Germany. Six months went by and then one day the doctor's wife called him at his office.

"Dear, you received a very strange post card in the mail today," she explained. "I don't understand what it means!"

It says, "SAUERKRAUT, SAUERKRAUT, SAUERKRAUT; TWO WITH WIENERS, ONE WITHOUT!"

A True Story (G)

Nike has a television commercial for hiking shoes that was shot in Kenya using Samburu tribesmen. The camera closes in on one tribesman who speaks in native Maa. As he speaks, the Nike slogan "Just Do It" appears on the screen.

An anthropologist at the University of Cincinatti, says the Kenyan is really saying, "I don't want these. Give me big shoes."

Says Nike's spokeswoman, "We thought nobody in America would know what he said."

First Time (PG-13)

After a few days on the new Earth, the Lord called to Adam and said, "It is time for you and Eve to begin the process of populating the earth, so I want you to kiss her."

Adam answered, "Yes, Lord, but what is a 'kiss'?" The Lord gave a brief description to Adam, who took Eve by the hand and took her to a nearby bush.

A few minutes later, Adam emerged and said, "Thank you Lord, that was enjoyable."

And the Lord replied, "Yes Adam, I thought you might enjoy that. Now, I'd like you to caress Eve."

And Adam said, "What is a 'caress'?"

So, the Lord again gave Adam a brief description and Adam went behind the bush with Eve.

Quite a few minutes later, Adam returned, smiling, and said, "Lord, that was even better than the kiss."

And the Lord said, "You've done well Adam. And now, I want you to make love to Eve."

And Adam asked, "What is 'make love', Lord?"

So, the Lord again gave Adam directions and Adam went again to Eve behind the bush, but this time he re-appeared in two seconds.

And Adam said, "Lord, what is a 'headache'?"

Love of Baseball (G)

You see, there were these two old men who loved baseball. They loved to go to games, watch games, listen to games on the radio, and talk baseball. However, they both knew they were reaching the end of their lives and thus decided to make a pact with each other. Whichever of the two was to die first, he would try to come back in some way and let the other know if there was baseball in heaven.

Well, as the story goes, one of the men soon took sick and passed away, leaving his friend alone. But not more than a week had passed since the funeral when a ghost appeared to the old man as he was watching the Red Sox-Yankees game. He looked closely and realized that it was indeed the ghost of his old friend. He had been able to come back!

"You've made it back!" said the old man.

"Yes, but I've got good news and bad news," said the ghost.

"Tell me, my friend, is there baseball in heaven?" said the old man.

"Well, yes, there is, that's the good news."

"Wonderful! Now, what's the bad news?"

"The bad news is...You're pitching tomorrow."

The Photographer (G)

The photographer for a national magazine was assigned to get photos of a great forest fire. Smoke at the scene was too thick to get any good shots, so he frantically called his home office to hire a plane. "It will be waiting for you at the airport!" he was assured by his editor.

As soon as he got to the small, rural airport, sure enough, a plane was warming up near the runway. He jumped in with his equipment and yelled,

"Lets go! Let's go!" The pilot swung the plane into the wind and soon they were in the air.

"Fly over the north side of the fire," said the photographer, "and make three or four low, level passes."

"Why?" asked the pilot.

"Because I'm going to take picture!" said the photographer with great exasperation. "I'm a photographer, and photographers take pictures!"

After a long pause the pilot said, "You mean you're not the instructor?"

Strip Club Birthday (PG-13)

Dave works hard at the plant and spends most evenings bowling or playing basketball at the gym. His wife thinks he is pushing himself too hard, so for his birthday she takes him to a local strip club.

The doorman at the club greets them and says, "Hey, Dave, how ya doin?"

His wife is puzzled and asks if he's been to this club before.

"Oh no," says Dave. "He's on my bowling team."

When they are seated, a waitress asks Dave if he'd like his usual Budweiser. His wife is becoming uncomfortable and says, "You must come here a lot for that woman to know you drink Budweiser".

"No, honey, she's in the Ladies Bowling League. We share lanes with them."

A stripper comes over to their table and throws her arms around Dave.

"Hi Davey," she says, "Want your usual table dance?"

Dave's wife, now furious, grabs her purse and storms out of the club. Dave follows and spots her getting into a cab. Before she can slam the door, he jumps in beside her and she starts screaming at him. The cabby turns his head and says, "Looks like you picked up a real bitch tonight, Dave."

The Race (G)

There was a young boy who lived about 30 miles from Houston, Texas. He decided he wanted to take a trip into the city by himself so he saved all his money.

When he had enough money he asked his mom if he could go. The day he left she packed him a lunch and off he rode on his bike. He had been pedaling for about 30 minutes when a guy in a Corvette drove alongside him.

guy: Where you going?

boy: I'm going to Houston.

guy: That's a long way to have to ride your bike, you want a ride?

boy: YEA, but what about my bike.

guy: Oh, hmm... I know, I have a tow rope in my trunk. I'll tie one end to your handle bars and the other to my bumper. If while I'm driving I go too fast, just ring the bell on your bike and I'll slow down.

boy: Hey, great. Let's go.

So off they go. The driver finally levels off at about 40 mph and everyone's happy. A few minutes later another guy in this BMW pulls up alongside the Corvette. He revs the engine, pulls ahead, drops back, pulls ahead again and starts yelling at the guy in the Corvette about his high performance 'vette only can do 40! Before you know both cars are gone in a cloud of dust. About 5 miles down the road they pass a speed trap.

Cop radioing ahead to his partner: "Larry, you're not going to believe this. A Corvette and BMW just passed me going 170 mph. They're heading your way, so be ready. And you want to hear the amazing part of it ... there's this little kid on a bike, ringing his bell for all its worth, trying to pass 'em."

The Rude Parrot (G)

A fellow buys a parrot, but the parrot's vocabulary is rude at best. The Fellow tries to reform his parrot by offering tidbits, shouts, and more, but nothing works.

Frustrated, he throws parrot into the freezer, and can still hear insults for a few minutes. But then there is a sudden silence. Worried that he's broken the bird, he whips open the freezer.

The parrot comes out with wholly-changed demeanor. It says:, "On reflection, my language has been improper. I intend to change. I beg your pardon."

There's a pause, then the parrot adds, "May I ask what, exactly, the turkey did?"

Voodoo Penis (R)

A businessman was getting ready to go on a long business trip. He knew his wife was a flirtatious sort with an extremely healthy sex drive, so he thought he'd buy her a little something to keep her occupied while he was gone.

He went to a store that sold sex toys and started to look around. He thought about a life-sized sex doll, but that was too close to another man for him. He was browsing through the dildo's, looking for something special to please his wife, and started talking to the old man behind the counter. He explained his situation.

"Well, I don't really know of anything that will do the trick. We have vibrating dildos, special attachments, and so on, but I don't know of thing that will keep her occupied for weeks, except..." and he stopped.

"Except what?" the man asked.

"Nothing, nothing."

"C'mon, tell me! I need something!"

"Well, sir, I don't usually mention this, but there is The Voodoo penis."

"So what's up with this Voodoo Penis?" he asked.

The old man reached under the counter, and pulled out a very old wooden box, carved with strange symbols and erotic images. He opened it, and there lay an ordinary-looking dildo. The businessman laughed, and said "Big damn deal. It looks like every other dildo in this shop!"

The old man replied, "But you haven't seen what it'll do yet."
He pointed to a door and said "Voodoo Penis, the door."

The Voodoo Penis miraculously rose out of its box, darted over to the door, and started pounding the keyhole. The whole door shook wildly with the vibrations, so much so that a crack began to form down the middle.

Before the door split, the old man said "Voodoo Penis, return to box!" The Voodoo Penis stopped, levitated back to the box and lay there quiescent once more.

"I'll take it!" said the businessman.

The old man resisted, saying it wasn't for sale, but finally surrendered to $738 in cash and an imitation Rolex.

The guy took it home to his wife, told her it was a special dildo and that to use it, all she had to do was say "Voodoo Penis, my crotch."

He left for his trip satisfied that things would be fine while he was gone. After he'd been gone a few days, his wife was unbearably horny. She thought of several people who would willingly satisfy her, but then she remembered the Voodoo Penis.

She undressed, opened the box and said, "Voodoo Penis, my crotch!" The Voodoo Penis shot to her crotch and started pumping. It was absolutely
incredible, like nothing she'd ever experienced before. After three mind-shattering orgasms, she became very exhausted and decided she'd had
enough.

She tried to pull it out, but it was stuck in her, still thrusting. She tried and tried to get it out, but nothing worked. Her husband had forgotten to tell her how to shut it off.

Worried, she decided to go to the hospital to see if they could help. She put her clothes on, got in the car and started to drive, quivering with every thrust of the dildo. On the way, another incredible intense orgasm made her swerve all over the road.

A police officer saw this and immediately pulled her over. He asked for her license, and then asked how much she'd had to drink.

Gasping and twitching, she explained, "I haven't had anything to drink,officer. You see, I've got this Voodoo Penis thing stuck in my crotch and it won't stop screwing me!"

The officer looked at her for a second, shook his head and in anarrogant voice replied, "Yeah, right... Voodoo Penis, my ass!"

Why You are So Tired (G)

For a couple years I've been blaming it on iron poor blood, lack of vitamins, dieting and a dozen other maladies. But now I found out the real reason. I'm tired because I'm overworked.

The population of this country is 237 million. 104 million are retired. That leaves 133 million to do the work.

There are 85 million in school, which leave 48 million to do the work.

Of this there are 29 million employed by the federal government. This leaves 19 million to do the work.

Four million are in the Armed Forces, which leaves 15 million to do the work.

Take from the total the 14,800,000 people who work for State and City Government and that leaves 200,000 to do the work.

There are 188,000 in hospitals, so that leaves 12,000 to do the work.

Now, there are 11,998 people in Prisons. That leaves Just two people to do the work.

You and me. And you're sitting there reading your E-mail.

Let's Hide In Here (G)
Larry Blanchfield, 31, an inmate serving a life term at the Delaware Correctional Center, was crushed to death when he tried to escape in a garbage truck. Authorities explained it is standard procedure for truck drivers to compact the trash they pick up before leaving the prison.

Why I Fired My Secretary (PG-13)
Two weeks ago was my forty-fifth birthday and I wasn't feeling too hot that morning anyway. I went in to breakfast knowing that my wife would be pleasant and say "Happy Birthday" and have a present for me. But she didn't even say "Good Morning" let alone say "happy birthday".

I thought to myself, "well that's a wife for you. The children will remember." The children came into breakfast and didn't say a word. And when I started to the office I was feeling pretty low and despondent.

As I walked into my office, Janet, my secretary, said "Good Morning, Boss, Happy Birthday," and I felt a little better that someone had remembered. I worked until noon. About noon she knocked on my door and said, "You know, it's such a beautiful day and it is your birthday, let's
go to lunch, just you and me." I said "By George, that's the greatest thing I've heard all day. Let's go."

We went to lunch. We didn't go where I normally go. We went out into the country to a little private place. We each had two martinis and enjoyed lunch tremendously. On the way back to the office she said, "You know, it's such a beautiful day and we do not need to go back to the office, do we?" I said "No, I guess not." She said, "Let's go by my apartment and I will fix you another martini."

We went to her apartment, we enjoyed another martini and smoked a cigarette, and she said "Boss, if you don't mind, I'll go into the bedroom and slip into something more comfortable," and I allowed her, as I didn't mind at all.

She went into the bedroom, and in six minutes she came out of the bedroom carrying a big birthday cake, followed by my wife and children. All were singing Happy Birthday. And there I was with nothing on but my socks.

First Time (G)

On his weekly visit to the general store in a small Idaho town, a farmer asked the grizzled proprietor for some dynamite to blast a few stumps from his fields. As the old-timer was getting the dynamite from the shelf, the farmer asked if he could have it put on his bill. "Well, friend," the proprietor said, "have you ever use this stuff before?"

"Why no, this will be the first time," the farmer replied.

"Then," said the old-timer, "I'm afraid I'll have to ask you to pay cash."

A Man, His Wife And The Cop (G)

A man seeing flashing red and blue lights in his rear view mirror pulls to the side of the road. A minute or so after coming to a stop, a police officer approaches the car.

The man says, "What's the problem officer?"

Officer: You were going 75 miles an hour in a 55 mile an hour zone. I'm afraid I'm going to have to ticket you.

Man: No sir, I was going a little over 60.

Wife: Oh, Harry. You were going at least 80! [The man gives wife dirty look.]

Officer: I'm also going to give you a ticket for your broken tail light.

Man: Broken tail light? I didn't know about a broken tail light!

Wife: Oh Harry, you've known about that tail light for weeks! [The man gives his wife another a dirty look.]

Officer: I'm also going to give you a citation for not wearing your seat belt.

Man: Oh, I just took it off when you were walking up to the car.

Wife: Oh, Harry, you never wear your seat belt!

The Man turns to his wife and yells, "For cryin' out loud, can't you just shut up?!"

The officer turns to the woman and asks, "Ma'am, Does your husband talk to you this way all the time?"

Wife says, "No officer, Only when he's drunk."

Hard Working People (G)

A man sees in the street two workers performing the following procedure: The first one is digging a ditch, and the second one, a few feet behind is covering the ditch with the the sand that was just dug out.

After watching them for a while he could not resist his curiosity and he went to ask them what they are doing and what was the goal in their work.

"This is very simple, mister" said one of the workers. "Usually we are a team of three: One digs, the other puts communication cable into the ditch and the third
one covers it. Unfortunately, the guy who puts the cables into the ditch is sick today, so we are doing the best we can."

The Pearly Gates (PG-13)

Three men die in a car accident on Christmas day. They all find themselves at the pearly gates waiting to enter Heaven. On entering they must present something Christmas like.

The first man searches his pocket, and finds some mistletoe, so he is allowed in. The second man presents a small wrapped present that was in his pocket, so he is also allowed in. The third man pulls out a pair of panties.

Confused at this last gesture , the angel asks "how do these represent Christmas?"

Answer: "they're Carol's."

Lucky Day (PG-13)

One morning, a man approached the first tee, only to find another guy approaching from the other side. They began talking and decided to play 9 holes together. After teeing off, they sat off down the fairway, continuing their chat.

"What do you do?" the first man asked.

"I'm a salesman. What about you?"

"I'm a hitman for the mob," replied the second man.

The hitman noticed that the 1st guy started getting a little nervous and continued. "Yeah. I'm the highest paid guy in the business. I'm the best." He stopped, sat down his bag of clubs, and pulled out a fancy, high powered rifle that was loaded with all types of scopes and sights. He than asked the man where he lived.

Still nervous the man replied, "In a subdivision just west of here."

The hitman placed the gun against his shoulder, faced west, peered into a scope and asked "What color roof ya' got?"

"Gray."

Then he asked "What color siding?"
"

"Yellow."

"You got a silver Toyota?"

"Yeah," replied the first man who was now completely amazed by the accuracy of the hitman's equipment. "That's my wife's car."

"That your red pickup next to it?"

Looking baffled the man asked if he could look through the scope. Looking through the sights, he said "Hell. That's my buddy Jeff's truck. What the hell is he doing there if I'm..?"

The hitman looked through the scope once more. "Your wife a blond?"

"Yeah."

"Your buddy got black hair?"

"Yeah!"

"Well, I don't know how to tell you, but I think you've got a problem. They're going at it like a couple of teenagers in there." said the hitman.

"Problem??! THEY'VE got the problem! I want you to shoot both of them! Right now!"

The hitman paused and said, "Sure. But it'll cost you. Like I said, I'm the best. I get paid $5,000 per shot."

"I don't care! Just do it! I want you to shoot her right in the head, then shoot him right in the balls!"

The hitman agreed, turned, and took firing position. He carefully stared into the sights, taking careful aim. He then said, "You know what buddy. This is your lucky day. I think I can save you $5,000!"

Darwin Award Candidate (G)

Doctors at Portland's University Hospital said an Oregon man shot through the skull by a hunting arrow is lucky to be alive, and will be released soon from the hospital. Mr. Roberts, 25, lost his right eye last weekend during an initiation into a men's rafting club, Mountain Men Anonymous, in Grants Pass, Ore. A friend tried to shoot a beer can off his head, but the arrow entered Roberts' right eye. Doctors said had the arrow gone 1 millimeter to the left, a major blood vessel would have been cut and Roberts would have died instantly. Neurosurgeon Dr. Johnny D. at the University Hospital in Portland said the arrow went through 8 to 10 inches of brain, with the tip protruding at the rear of his skull, yet somehow managed to miss all major blood vessels.

The Doctor also said had Robert tried to pull the arrow out on his own he surely would have killed himself. Mr. Robert admitted afterwards he and his friends had been drinking that afternoon. Said Roberts, "I feel so dumb about this." No charges have been filed but the Josephine County district attorney's office said the initiation stunt is under investigation.

How to Decipher Employment Want Ads Terminology (G)

Energetic self-starter: You'll be working on commission.
Entry level position: We will pay you the lowest wages allowed by law.
Experience required: We do not know the first thing about any of this.
Fast learner: You will get no training from us.
Flexible work hours: You will frequently work long overtime hours.
Make an investment in you future: This is a franchise or a pyramid scheme.
Management training position: You'll be a salesperson with a wide territory.
Must be able to lift 50 pounds: We offer no health insurance or chiropractors.
Opportunity of a lifetime: You will not find a lower salary for so much work.
Quick problem solver: You will work on projects months behind schedule already.
Strong communication skills: You will write tons of documentation and letters.

Paperless Submarine (G)

Spotted in a recent "New Scientist" article on 'the paperless office': A modern U.S. Navy Submarine now requires 26 tons of manuals. This is enough to affect the vessel's performance.

How Men Think (R)

A man is visiting his wife in hospital where she has been in a coma for several years. On this visit he decides to rub her left breast instead of just talking to her. On doing this she lets out a sigh. The man runs out and tells the doctor who says this is a good sign and suggests he should try rubbing her right breast to see if there is any reaction. The man goes in and rubs her right breast and this brings a moan from his wife. He rushes out and tells the doctor. The doctor says this is amazing and is a real break through. The doctor then suggests the man should go in and try oral sex, saying he will wait outside as it is a personal act and he doesn't want the man to be embarrassed. The man goes in then comes out about five minutes later, white as a sheet and tells the doctor his wife is dead. The doctor asks what happened to which the man replies "She choked."

Skirt Too Tight (PG-13)

One day, a large group of people were waiting for the bus at a localGreyhound station. At the front of the line was a very attractivewoman dressed in a black business vest, white blouse, leatherminiskirt, and high heels.

As the bus pulled up and opened the door, she went to board it, but found that her skirt was too tight for her to raise her leg to the required height. Looking around and thinking quickly, she reaches behind her and undoes the zipper on the back of her skirt a little and then tries again.

Again, she finds that she cannot manage the step, so once more shereaches behind her and unzips her skirt a little more. With a smile, she looks at the bus driver and tries to board again. She finds that she still can't step that high and so with exasperation and a sigh she unzips her skirt the rest of the way down. To her amazement, her leg still will not reach the bottom step.

Finally, a very large Texan behind her gently grabs her by the waist, lifts her up, and places her on the bus.

The woman turns to the Texan furious and says, "Who do you think you are to touch my body in that way? I don't even know you!"

The Texan looks at her and replies, "Well, ma'am, after you unzipped my fly I thought we were pretty good friends."

Holiday in Pakistan (PG-13)

A married couple is on holiday in Pakistan. They're touring around the marketplace looking at the goods and such, when they pass this small sandal shop. From inside they hear a gentleman with a Pakistani accent say, "You, foreigners! Come in, come into my humble shop. Salaam a leekem! (hello in English)"

So the married couple walks in. The Pakistani man says to them, "I have some special sandals I think you'd be interested in. They make you wild at sex like a great desert camel."

Well, the wife, after hearing this, is really interested in buying the sandals, but her husband feels he really doesn't need them, being the sex god he is.

The husband tells the man, "How could sandals make you into a sex freak?"

The Pakistani man replies "Just try them on."

Well, the husband, after much badgering from his wife, finally concedes to try them on. The husband puts them on and gets this wild look in his eyes, something his wife has not seen in many years, raw sexual power.

In a blink of the eye, the husband rushes the Pakistani man, throws him on a table and starts tearing at the guy's pants. All the time the Pakistani man is screaming, "No, no, no! You've got them on the wrong feet!"

Two Nuns On Bikes (PG-13)

Two Italian nuns are riding their rickety old bikes down the back streets of Rome one late afternoon. As it turns dusk, the increasing darkness starts making one of the nuns a little nervous. She leans over to the other and says, "You know, I've never come this way before."

The other nun replies, "It's the cobblestones."

Great Comeback (PG-13)

An award should go to the United Airlines gate agent in Denver for being smart and funny, and making her point, when confronted with a passenger who probably deserved to fly cargo.

During the final days at Denver's old Stapleton Airport, a crowded United flight was canceled. A single agent was rebooking a long line of inconvenienced travelers. Suddenly an angry passenger pushed his way to the desk. He slapped his ticket down on the counter and said, " I HAVE to be on this flight and it has to be FIRST CLASS."

The agent replied, "I'm sorry, sir. I'll be happy to try to help you, but I've got to help these folks first, and I'm sure we'll be able to work something out."

The passenger was unimpressed. He asked loudly, so that the passengers behind him could hear, "Do you have any idea who I am?"

Without hesitating, the gate agent smiled and grabbed her public address microphone, "May I have your attention please?" she began, her voice bellowing throughout the terminal. "We have a passenger here at the gate WHO DOES NOT KNOW WHO HE IS. If anyone can help him find his identity, please come to the gate."

With all the folks behind him in line laughing hysterically, the man glared at the United agent, gritted his teeth and swore, "f*ck you."

Without flinching, she smiled and said, "I'm sorry sir, but you will have to stand in line for that, too."

The man retreated as the people in the terminal applauded loudly. Although the flight was canceled and the people were late, they were no longer angry at United.

Rednecks Going Camping (G)

Two rednecks go on a fishing trip. They rent all the equipment - the reels, the rods, the wading suits, the rowboat, the car, and even a cabin in the woods. I mean they spend a fortune!

The first day they go fishing, but they don't catch anything. The same thing happens on the second day, and on the third day. It goes on like this until finally, on the last day of their vacation, one of the men catches a fish.

As they're driving home they're really depressed. One guy turns to the other and says, "Do you realize that this one lousy fish we caught cost us fifteen hundred bucks?"

The other guy says, "Wow! Then it's a good thing we didn't catch any more!"

Good Example (G)

Little Johnnie was late for class, and when he saw that the door was already closed, he opened it and went into the classroom tentatively. He very quietly shut the door and tiptoed to his seat hoping not to get the teacher after him.

This upset the teacher, who said him, "Johnnie, is this how your father would have come in - late and sneaking to his seat? Go out and try it again, and get it right this time!"

So, Little Johnnie left the room and shut the door behind him quietly, as he'd come in. Then a moment later, he flung open the door with a clatter and stomped back into the room with a lit cigarette dangling from his lips. He slammed the door behind him, put his cigarette out on the carpet with his foot and said, "So Honey, didn't expect ME, did ya?"

The Real Men Test (PG-13)

Note: All "real men" answer "C" to all of these questions.

1. Alien beings from a highly advanced society visit the Earth, and you are the first human they encounter. As a token of intergalactic friendship, they present you with a small but incredibly sophisticated device that is capable of curing all disease, providing an infinite supply of clean energy, wiping out hunger and poverty, and permanently eliminating oppression and violence all over the entire Earth. You decide to:
   A. Present it to the President of the United States.
   B. Present it to the Secretary General of the United Nations.
   C. Take it apart.

2. When is it okay to kiss another male?
   A. When you wish to display simple and pure affection without regard for narrow-minded social conventions.
   B. When he is the Pope. (Not on the lips.)
   C. When he is your brother and you are Al Pacino and this

is the only really sportsman-like way to let him know that, for business reasons, you have to have him killed.

3. In your opinion, the ideal pet is:
   A. A cat.
   B. A dog.
   C. A dog that eats cats.

4. You have been seeing a woman for several years. She's attractive and intelligent, and you always enjoy being with her. One leisurely Sunday afternoon the two of you are taking it easy you're watching a football game; she's reading the papers when she suddenly, but of the clear blue sky, tells you that she thinks she really loves you, but, she can no longer bear the uncertainty of not knowing where your relationship is going. She says she's not asking whether you want to get married; only whether you believe that you have some kind of future together. What do you say?

A. That you sincerely believe the two of you do have a future, but you don't want to rush it.
B. That although you also have strong feelings for her, you can not honestly say that you'll be ready anytime soon to make a lasting commitment, and you don't want to hurt her by holding out false hope.
C. That you cannot believe the Broncos called a draw play on third and seventeen.

5. Okay, so you have decided that you truly love a woman and you want to spend the rest of your life with her, sharing the joys and the sorrows the world has to offer, come what may. How do you tell her?
   A. You take her to a nice restaurant and tell her after dinner.
   B. You take her for a walk on a moonlit beach, and you say her name, and when she turns to you, with the sea breeze blowing her hair and the stars in her eyes, you tell her.

C. Tell her what?

6. When is it okay to throw away a set of veteran underwear?
   A. When it has turned the color of a dead whale and developed new holes so large that you're not sure which ones were originally intended for your legs.
   B. When it is down to eight loosely connected underwear molecules and has to be handled with tweezers.
   C. It is never okay to throw away veteran underwear. A real guy checks the garbage regularly in case somebody and we are not naming names, but this would be his wife is quietly trying to discard his underwear (which she is frankly jealous of because the guy seems to have a more intimate relationship with it than with her).

7. What, in your opinion, is the most reasonable explanation for the fact that Moses led the Israelites all over the place for forty years before they finally got to the Promised Land?
   A. He was being tested.
   B. He wanted them to really appreciate the Promised Land when they finally got there.
   C. He refused to ask for directions.

Smart Aleck (PG-13)

"If there are 4 birds on a fence and you shoot one, how many birds are left on the fence?" Johnny replies, "None, because after I shoot the first bird, the others will fly away." The teacher says, "Well, the correct answer is 'three birds', but I like your thinking." So Johnny says, "Well I have a question for you... There are three women in an ice cream shop eating ice cream cones. The first woman is licking the cone. The second woman is biting the cone. And the third woman is sucking the cone. Which one is married?" The teacher replies, "I don't know. I guess the one that is sucking the cone." To which

Johnny says, "Well the correct answer is the one with the wedding ring', but I like your thinking."

Halloween Party (PG-13)
A couple was invited to a swanky masked Halloween Party. The wife came down with a terrible headache and told her husband to go to the party alone. He, being a devoted husband, protested, but she argued and said she was going to take some aspirin and go to bed, and there was no need of his good time being spoiled by not going. So he took his costume and away he went.

The wife, after sleeping soundly for one hour, awakened without pain, and as it was still early, she decided to go to the party. In as much as her husband did not know what her costume was, she thought she would have some fun by watching her husband to see how he acted when she was not with him.

She joined the party and soon spotted her husband cavorting around on the dance floor, dancing with every woman he could find, and copping a little feel here and a little kiss there. His wife sidled up to him and being a rather seductive babe herself he left his partner high and dry and devoted his time to the new stuff that had just arrived.

She let him go as far as he wished; naturally, since he was her husband. Finally he whispered a little proposition in her ear and she agreed, so off they went to
one of the cars and had a little fun. Just before unmasking at midnight, she slipped away and went home and put the costume away and got into bed, wondering what kind of explanation he would make for his behavior.

She was sitting up reading when he came in and asked what kind of a time he had. He said, "Oh, the same old thing. You know I never have a good time when you're not there."

Then she asked, "Did you dance much?"

He replied, "I'll tell you, I never even danced one dance.

When I got there, I met Pete, Bill Brown and some other guys, so we went into the den and played poker all evening. But I'll tell you... the guy I loaned my costume to sure had a real good time!"

The Quickest Way (G)

Fortune Magazine reported that some employees of Merrill Lynch's New York office were so incensed at its mailroom service a few years ago that they sent interoffice mail via Federal Express. "Memos were whisked from floor to floor via Memphis."

A Bargain (R)

A couple, both 67, went to a sex therapist's office. The doctor asked, "What can I do for you?" The man said, "Will you watch us have sexual intercourse?"

The doctor looked puzzled, but agreed. The doctor examined them and then directed them to disrobe and go at it. When the couple finished, the doctor reexamined them and, upon completion, advised the couple, "There's nothing wrong with the way you have intercourse." He then charged them $32.

This happened several weeks in a row. The couple would make an appointment, have intercourse with no apparent problems other than the lack of vigor which is to be expected in 67 year olds, get dressed, pay the doctor, and then leave.

Finally after almost two months of this routine, the doctor asked, "Just exactly what are you trying to find out?"

The old man said, "Oh, we're not trying to find out anything. She's married and we can't go to her house. I'm married, so we can't go to my house. The Holiday Inn charges $60.

The Hilton charges $78. We do it here for $32 and I get $28 back from Medicaid.

Oreo Cookie Personality Test (PG-13)

Psychologists have discovered that the manner in which people eat Oreo cookies provides great insight into their personalities. Choose which method best describes your favorite method of eating Oreo's:
1. The whole thing all at once.
2. One bite at a time.
3. Slow and methodical nibbles examining the results of each bite afterwards.
4. In little feverous nibbles.
5. Dunked in some liquid (milk, coffee...).
6. Twisted apart, the inside, then the cookie.
7. Twisted apart, the inside, and toss the cookie.
8. Just the cookie, not the inside.
9. I just like to lick them, not eat them.
10. I don't have a favorite way because I don't like Oreo.

Put your answers down now, then check below:
Your Personality:
1. The whole thing: This means you consume life with abandon, you are fun to be with, exciting, carefree with some hint of recklessness. You are totally irresponsible. No one should trust you with their children.
2. One bite at a time. You are lucky to be one of the 5.4 billion other people who eat their Oreo's this very same way. Just like them, you lack imagination, but that's OK, not to worry, you're normal.
3. Slow and Methodical. You follow the rules. You're very tidy and orderly. You're very meticulous in every detail with every thing you do to the point of being anal retentive and irritating to others. Stay out of the fastlane if

you're only going to go the speed limit.
4. Feverous Nibbles. Your boss likes you because you get your work done quickly. You always have a million things to do and never enough time to do them. Mental break downs and suicides run in your family. Valium and Ritalin would do you good.
5. Dunked. Every one likes you because you are always up beat. You like to sugar coat unpleasant experiences and rationalize bad situations into good ones. You are in total denial about the shambles you call a life. You have a propensity towards narcotic addiction.
6. Twisted apart, the inside, and then the cookie. You have a highly curious nature. You take pleasure in breaking things apart to find out how they work, though not always able to put them back together, so you destroy all the evidence of your activities. You deny your involvement when things go wrong. You are a compulsive liar and exhibit deviant, if not criminal, behavior.
7. Twisted apart, the inside, and then toss the cookie. You are good at business and take risk that pay off. You take what you want and throw the rest away. You are greedy, selfish, mean, and lack feelings for others. You should be ashamed of yourself. But that's OK, you don't care, you got yours.
8. Just the cookie, not the inside. You enjoy pain.
9. I just like to lick them, not eat them. Stay away from small furry animals and seek professional medical help- immediately.
10 I don't have a favorite way, I don't like Oreo cookies. You probably come from a rich family, and like to wear nice things, and go to upscale restaurants. You are particular and fussy about the things you buy, own, and wear. Things have to be just right. You like to be pampered. You are a primadona. There's just no pleasing you.

Three Wise Women (G)
You do know what would have happened if it had been three wise WOMEN instead of men, don't you?

They would have asked for directions, arrived on time, helped deliver the baby, cleaned the stable, made a casserole and brought practical gifts.

Federal Employee and the Genie (G)
A Federal Government Employee sits in his office and out of boredom, decides to see what's in his old filing cabinet. He pokes through the contents and comes across an old brass lamp. "This will look nice on my mantelpiece," he decides, and takes it home with him. While polishing the lamp, a genie appears and grants him three wishes.

"I wish for an ice cold diet Pepsi right now!" He gets his Pepsi and drinks it. Now that he can think more clearly, he states his second wish.

"I wish to be on an island where beautiful nymphomaniacs reside." Suddenly he is on an island with gorgeous females eyeing him lustfully.

He tells the genie his third and last wish: "I wish I'd never have to work ever again."

POOF! He's back in his government office.

Double Ouch (PG-13)
DETROIT -- A man who went to a chiropractic clinic last month for treatment of a sore back ended up with another kind of pain when he got his genitals caught in a folding exam table. Now, James V. is suing seeking damages for pain and suffering, disfigurement and for consequential damages -- such as the lack of sexual performance or enjoyment. He said

he went to the clinic and the chiropractor had him take off his clothes and lie face down on a table. He said his genitals fell between two parts of the table, and when the chiropractor adjusted the table, he got caught! "I got off of the table and I went down to my knees," A clinic employee drove him to a hospital, where a small part of damaged skin had to be removed. His lawyer expects a settlement to the lawsuit to exceed "six figures."

The Modern Hunters (G)

A guy buys a brand new Jeep Grand Cherokee for $30,000+, and has $400.00+ in monthly payments. He's pretty proud of this rig, gets a hold of his friend to do some male bonding with the new ride. They go duck hunting and of course all the lakes are frozen. These two Atomic Brains go to the lake with their guns, the dog, the beer they picked up and of course the new vehicle. They drive out onto the ice. Now, they want to make some kind of a natural landing area to attract ducks. Remember it's all ice, and in order to make a hole large enough to interest a flock of ducks - a hole big enough to entice ducks to land, they needed to use a little more than an ice hole drill. So, out of the back of the brand-new Jeep Grand Cherokee comes a stick of dynamite with a short 40-Second fuse. Now to their credit, these two rocket scientists DID take into consideration that if they placed the stick of dynamite on the ice at a location far from where they (and the new Grand Cherokee) would be waiting, and ran back quickly, they would risk slipping on the ice as they ran from the imminent explosion, and could possibly go up in smoke with the resulting blast.

After a little deliberation, they come up with lighting and THROWING the dynamite, which is what they end up doing. Remember a couple of paragraphs back when I mentioned the vehicle, the beer, the guns AND THE DOG???? Yes, the dog.

The driver's pet Black Lab (used for retrieving -especially things thrown by the owner). You guessed it, the dog takes off at a high rate of doggy speed on the ice, reaching the stick of dynamite with the burning 40 second fuse about the time it hits the ice - all to the woe of the two idiots which are now yelling, stomping, waving arms and wondering what the heck to do now?! The dog is happy and now heads back toward the "hunters" with the stick of dynamite. I think we all can picture the ever-increasing concern on the part of the brain trust, as the loyal Labrador Retriever approaches.

The Bozos now are REALLY waving their arms - yelling even louder and generally feeling kinda panicked. Now finally one of the guys decides to think - something that neither had done before this moment, grabs a shotgun and shoots the dog.

This sounds better than it really is, because the shotgun was loaded with #8 duck shot and hardly effective enough to stop a Black Lab. The dog DID stop for a moment, slightly confused, but then continued on.

Another shot, and this time the dog - still standing, became REALLY confused and of course scared. TOTALLY INSANE, the pooch takes off to find cover with a now extremely short fuse still burning on the stick of dynamite. The cover the dogs finds? Underneath the brand new Grand Cherokee worth 30-some thousand dollars, the $400.00+ monthly payment vehicle that is sitting nearby on the lake ice. BOOM!! Dog dies, vehicle sinks to bottom of lake, and these two "Co-Leaders of the Known Universe" are left standing there with this "I can't EVEN believe this happened to me" look on their faces. Later, the owner of the vehicle calls his insurance company and is promptly informed that sinking a vehicle in a lake by illegal use of explosives is NOT covered on his policy. He had yet to make his first car payment.

How Eve Came About (G)

Adam was walking around the garden of Eden feeling very lonely, so God asked him, "What is wrong with you?" Adam said he didn't have anyone to talk to. God said that he was going to make Adam a companion and that it would be a woman. He said, "This person will gather food for you, cook for you, when you discover clothing, she'll wash it for you. She will always agree with every decision you make. She will bear your children and never ask you to get up in the middle of the night to take care of them. She will not nag you, and will always be the first to admit she was wrong when you've had a disagreement. She will never have a headache, and will freely give you love and passion whenever you need it." Adam asked God, "What will a woman like this cost?" God replied, "An arm and a leg." Then Adam asked, "What can I get for a rib?" The rest is history.

Bad Sex in Alabama (PG-13)

An elderly couple was driving cross country, the woman was driving. She gets pulled over by the highway patrol.

The patrolman says, "Ma'am did you know you were speeding?" The woman turns to her husband and asks, "What did he say?" The old man yells, "HE SAYS YOU WERE SPEEDING."

The patrolman says, "May I see your license?"

The woman turns to her husband and asks, "What did he say?"

The old man yells, "HE WANTS TO SEE YOUR LICENSE."

The woman gives him her license.

The patrolman says, "I see you are from Alabama. I spent some time there once, had the worst sex with a woman I had ever had."

The woman turns to her husband and asks, "What did he say?"

The old man yells, "HE THINKS HE KNOWS YOU."

By The Balls (PG-13)

A little old lady entered the main branch of the Chase Manhattan bank with a large grocery bag in her arms. She told the teller that she wanted to open an account to make a substantial deposit, in excess of $200,000.

Further, she said that since such a large sum was involved, she would deal only with the president of the bank to make the necessary arrangements.

The teller looked in the bag and confirmed that it was, in fact, full of cash. He called upstairs and explained the situation to the bank president, who agreed to see the woman. The teller escorted her to the president's office, and the president invited her to have a seat, which she accepted. She repeated her request to open an account.

The president said he would take care of it personally, but his curiosity was killing him. He said, "Mind if I ask how you happened to come into such a large sum of cash?"

"Not at all," was her reply. "I bet."

"You bet?" he countered. "At the racetrack, or on professional sports, or in casinos ...?"

"Nothing like that," she said. "I just ... bet. For example, I'll bet you $50,000 that by tomorrow morning your balls will be square."

The president chuckled but, seeing that the lady was serious, and had the funds to back up such a wild bet, agreed. They shook hands on it, and she promised to return at nine the next morning to follow up, and left.

As the day wore on, the president found himself frequently checking to make sure that all was in order. It was, but just as a precaution he canceled his regular Tuesday-afternoon golf match and went home early. The next morning when he showered, he was actually relieved to find that nothing had changed drastically while he slept. He confidently headed for the bank, laughing all the way at the unexpected windfall that was about to become his.

The little old lady showed up promptly at the appointed hour, accompanied by a young man. When the president asked who he was, she replied that he was her lawyer, who she always brought along when payoffs involving significant sums were involved. The president told her that sorry, she had lost that particular bet, so the funds would be outgoing rather than incoming. She insisted on examining the evidence for herself, considering the amount at stake. He deemed it a reasonable request under the circumstances, so he stood up, unbuckled his belt and dropped his pants. She proceeded to closely inspect his jewels for any abnormalities.

As she did, the president noticed that her lawyer was standing in the corner, banging his head against the wall.

He asked the lady, "What's the matter with him?"

She replied, "Oh, him. I bet him $150,000 that before ten a.m. today I'd have the president of the Chase Manhattan Bank by the balls..."

Broken Engagement (G)

The soldier serving overseas, far from home was annoyed and upset when his girl wrote breaking off their engagement and asking for her photograph back.

He went out and collected from his friends all the unwanted photographs of women that he could find, bundled them all together and sent them back with a note saying: "Regret cannot remember which one is you-please keep your photo and return the others."

THE PERFECT DAY - FOR HER (G)

8:15 Wake up to hugs and kisses
8:30 Weigh in 2Kg lighter than yesterday
8:45 Breakfast in bed, freshly squeezed orange juice and croissants; open presents - expensive jewelry chosen by

thoughtful partner
9:15 Soothing hot bath with frangipani bath oil
10:00 Light work out at club with handsome funny personal trainer
10:30 Facial, manicure, shampoo, condition, blow dry
12:00 Lunch with best friend at fashionable outdoor cafe
12:45 Catch sight of husband/boyfriend's ex and notices she has gained 7kg
1:00 Shopping with friends, unlimited credit
3:00 Nap
4:00 Three dozen roses delivered by florist, card is from secret admirer
4:15 Light work out at club, followed by massage from strong but gentle hunk who says he rarely gets to work on such a perfect body
5.30 Choose outfit from expensive designer wardrobe, parade before full length mirror
7:30 Candle lit dinner for two followed by dancing, with compliments received from other diners/dancers
10:00 Hot shower (alone)
10:50 Carried to bed . . . (freshly ironed, crisp, new, white linen)
11:00 Pillow talk, light touching and cuddling
11:15 Fall asleep in his big strong arms

Perfume Wars (G)

A young and beautiful woman gets into the elevator, smelling like expensive perfume. She turns to an old woman and says arrogantly, "Giorgio Beverly Hills, $100 an ounce!"
Another young and beautiful woman gets on the elevator and also smells of very expensive perfume. She arrogantly turns to the old woman and says, "Chanel No. 5, $150 an ounce!"

About three floors later, the old woman has reached her destination and is about to get off the elevator. Before she leaves, looks both beautiful women in the eye, turns and bends

over, and farts.......
"Broccoli - 49 cents a pound."

This is Good (G)

The story is told of a king in Africa who had a close friend with whom he grew up. The friend had a habit of looking at every situation that ever occurred in his life (positive or negative) and remarking, "This is good!"

One day the king and his friend were out on a hunting expedition. The friend would load and prepare the guns for the king. The friend had apparently done something wrong in the preparation of one of the guns, for after taking the gun from his friend, the king fired it and his thumb was blown off. Examining the situation the friend remarked as usual, "This is good!" To which the king replied, "No, this is NOT good!" and proceeded to send his friend to jail. About a year later, the king was hunting in the area that he should have known to stay clear of. Cannibals captured him and took him to their village. They tied his hands, stacked some wood, set up a stake and bound him to the stake. As they came near to set fire to the wood, they noticed the king was missing a thumb. Being superstitious, they never ate anyone who was less than whole. So, untying the king they sent him on his way.

As he returned home, he was reminded of the event that had taken his thumb and felt remorse for the treatment of his friend. He went immediately to the jail to speak with his friend. "You were right," he said, "it was good that my thumb was blown off." And he proceeded to tell the friend all that had happened. "And so I am very sorry for sending you to jail for so long. It was bad of me to do this."

"No", the friend replied, "This is good!"

"What do you mean, 'This is good'? How could it be good that I sent my friend to jail for a year?" asked the bewildered king.

"If I had not been in jail, I would have been with you."

Funny Epitaphs from Real Tombstones (G)

Memory of an accident in a Uniontown, Pennsylvania cemetery: Here lies the body of Jonathan Blake-Stepped on the gas Instead of the brake.

In a Silver City, Nevada, cemetery: Here lays Butch, We planted him raw. He was quick on the trigger, But slow on the draw.

A widow wrote this epitaph in a Vermont cemetery: Sacred to the memory of my husband John Barnes who died January 3, 1803 His comely young widow, aged 23, has many qualifications of a good wife, and yearns to be comforted.

Someone determined to be anonymous in Stowe, Vermont: I was somebody. Who, is no business Of yours.

In a Georgia cemetery: "I told you I was sick!"

John Penny's epitaph in the Wimborne, England, cemetery: Reader if cash thou art, In want of any Dig 4 feet deep And thou wilt find a Penny.

On Margaret Daniels grave at Hollywood Cemetery Richmond, Virginia: She always said her feet were killing her but nobody believed her.

Anna Hopewell's grave in Enosburg Falls, Vermont: Here lies the body of our Anna Done to death by a banana it wasn't the fruit that laid her low but the skin of the thing that made her go.

A consumer tip from the grave of Ellen Shannon in Girard, Pennsylvania: Who was fatally burned March 21, 1870 by the explosion of a lamp filled with "R.E. Danforth's Non-Explosive Burning Fluid"

Harry Edsel Smith of Albany, New York made a fatal mistake: Born 1903--Died 1942 Looked up the elevator shaft to see if the car was on the way down. It was.

Fair warning from a Thurmont, Maryland, cemetery: Here

lies an Atheist, All dressed up And no place to go.

The Pearly Gates (G)

A guy arrives at the pearly gates, waiting to be admitted. St. Peter is leafing through the Big Book to see if the guy is worthy of entering.

After several minutes, St. Peter closes the book, furrows his brow, and says, "I don't really see that you ever really did anything great in your life, but I don't see anything really bad either." "Tell you what," St. Peter says. "If you can tell me of one REALLY good deed you did in your life, I'll let you in."

The guy thinks for a moment and says, "OK, well there was this one time when I was driving down the highway, and I saw a gang assaulting this poor girl. I slowed down, and sure enough, there they were, about 50 of em torturing this woman. Infuriated, I got out my car, grabbed a tire iron out of my trunk, and walked straight up to the leader of the gang. He was a huge guy with a studded leather jacket and a chain running from his nose to his ear. As I walked up to the leader, the gang members formed a circle around me." "So, I ripped the leader's chain out of his face and smashed him over the head with the tire iron," the guy says. "Then I turned around and yelled to the rest of them, 'Leave this poor, innocent girl alone! You're all a bunch of sick, deranged animals! Go home before I really teach you all a lesson in pain!'"

St. Peter, duly impressed, says "Wow! When did this happen?"

"Just a couple of minutes ago."

Dumb and Dumber (G)

I am a medical student currently doing a rotation in toxicology at the poison control center. Today, this woman called in very upset because she caught her little daughter eating ants. I quickly reassured her that the ants are not harmful and there would be no need to bring her daughter into the hospital. She calmed down, and at the end of the conversation happened to mention that she gave her daughter some ant poison to eat in order to kill the ants. I told her that she better bring her daughter in to the Emergency room right away.

Nymphomaniac (PG-13)

The woman seated herself in the psychiatrists office. "What seems to be the problem?" the doctor asked. "Well, I, uh," she stammered. "I think I, uh, might be a nymphomaniac."

"I see," he said. "I can help you, but I must advise you that my fee is $80 an hour."

"That's not bad," she replied. "How much for all night?"

Darwin Award (G)

Top honors for "Human Projectile of the Month" go to an unidentified dude who, I am told, is also a serious contender for the annual Darwin Award. That prestigious prize is given posthumously to the person who does the human gene pool the greatest service by removing himself from it in the most extraordinarily stupid fashion.

Troopers from the Arizona Highway Patrol got onto this gallant if not brainless form of ballistic research after motorists reported some mysterious scorched and blackened scars on a stretch of deserted highway. The more officers found, the stranger the case got. Here is what they kinda "pieced" together. JATO units are basically huge canisters of solid rocket fuel used to achieve "Jet Assisted Take Off", typically lifting big transport airplanes into the air from short, rough ground runways, or shooting overloaded planes from the decks of aircraft carriers.

They were not, repeat NOT, designed to augment the inherent boost factor of a 1967 Chevy Impala. But it is guessed that-let's call him Zippy-didn't know that when he hooked one up to his ride. Ol' Zip apparently chose his runway carefully, selecting a nice long, lonely piece of straight as a string highway in good repair. Not guessing he might need a bit more than five miles of zoom surface, Zippy's test track had, that far down the track, a gentle rise on a sloping turn. Anyways, the Zipster kicked the tire, lit the fire, and ran his Chev up to top cruising speed. And then hit the ignition! Investigators know exactly where this happened, judging from the extended patch of burned and melted asphalt. The pocket calculator boys figure Zip reached maximum thrust within five seconds, punching that Chevy up to "well in excess of 350 miles per hour" and continued at "full burn" for another 20 to 25 seconds. Early in that little sprint, at roughly 2.5 miles down the road, the Human Hydro Shock stood on the brakes, melting them completely, blowing the tires and rapidly reducing all four skins to liquefied trails on the pavement.

Remember that little rise on the turn? That's where Zippy concluded his land speed record attempt and went for airborne honors, ultimately reaching an altitude of 125 feet and still climbing when his flight was abruptly terminated. We'll never know how far or how high the Zipster might have gone. A cliff face of solid rock kind of got in his way, posing a serious reaffirmation of the law of physics vis-a-vis two chunks of matter cannot occupy the same space at the same time. Zip gave it hell though, blasting a six-foot crater in the Terra-verry-firma. The best modern forensic science could do was ID the car's make and model year. As for Da' big 'Z', only trace evidence of bone, teeth, and hair were found in the crater. If there isn't room in the Guinness Book of World Records for this one, there should at least be an honorable mention.

Guys at a Bar (PG-13)

Two guys wandered into a bar. One of the men shouted to the barkeeper, "Hiya, Mike. Set 'em up for me and my pal here." Then he turned to his slightly dim partner and boasted, "This is a great bar. For every two drinks you buy, the house gives you one. And the pinball machines in the back are free!"

"That's not so great, responded the friend. There's a bar across town that'll match you drink for drink, and you can get laid in the back for free."

"Where is this place?" the first guy exclaimed. "Oh, I don't know," the dim fellow replied, "but my wife goes there all the time."

True Stories (G)

Seems that a year ago, some Boeing employees on the field decided to steal a life raft from one of the 747s. They were successful in getting it out of the plane and home. When they took it for a float on the River, they were quite surprised by a Coast Guard helicopter coming towards them.

It turned out that the chopper was homing in on the emergency locator that is activated when the raft is inflated. They are no longer employed there.

A police officer had a perfect hiding place for watching for speeders. But one day, everyone was under the speed limit, the officer found the problem: a 10 year old boy was standing on the side of the road with a huge hand painted sign which said "RADAR TRAP AHEAD." A little more investigative work led the officer to the boy's accomplice, another boy about 100 yards beyond the radar trap with a sign reading, "TIPS" and a bucket at his feet, full of change.

A true story out of San Francisco: A man, wanting to rob a downtown Bank of America, walked into the branch and wrote "this iz a stikkup. Put all your muny in this bag." While standing in line, waiting to give his note to the teller, he began to worry that someone had seen him write the note and might call the police before he reached the teller window. So he left the Bank of America and crossed the street to Wells Fargo. After Waiting a few minutes in line, he handed his note to the Wells Fargo teller. She read it and, surmising from his spelling errors that he was not the brightest light in the harbor, told him that she could not accept his stickup note because it was written on a Bank of America deposit slip and that he would either have to fill out a Wells Fargo deposit slip or go back to Bank of America. Looking somewhat defeated, the man said "OK" and left. The Wells Fargo teller then called the police who arrested the man a few minutes later, as he was waiting in line back at Bank of America.

A motorist was unknowingly caught in an automated speed trap that measured his speed using radar and photographed his car. He later received in the mail a ticket for $40 and a photo of his car. instead of payment, he sent the police department a photograph of $40. Several days later, he received a letter from the police that contained another picture - of handcuffs.

A woman was reporting her car as stolen, and mentioned that there was a car phone in it. The policeman taking the report called the phone and told the guy that answered that he had read the ad in the newspaper and wanted to buy the car. They arranged to meet, and the thief was arrested.

Drug Possession Defendant Christopher Jansen, on trial in March in Pontiac, Michigan, said he had been searched without a warrant. The prosecutor said the officer didn't need a warrant because a "bulge" in Christopher's jacket could have been a gun. Nonsense, said Christopher, who happened to be wearing the same jacket that day in court. He handed it over so the judge could see it. The judge discovered a packet of cocaine in the pocket and laughed so hard he required a five minute recess to compose himself.

Oklahoma City: Dennis Newton was on trial for the armed robbery of a convenience store in a district court when he fired his lawyer. Assistant district attorney Larry Jones said Newton, 47, was doing a fair job of defending himself until the store manager testified that Newton was the robber. Newton jumped up, accused the woman of lying and then said, "I should of blown your (expletive) head off." The defendant paused, then quickly added, "if I'd been the one that was there." The jury took 20 minutes to convict Newton and recommended a 30 year sentence.

R.C. Gaitlan, 21, walked up to two patrol officers who were showing their squad car computer equipment to children in a Detroit neighborhood. When he asked how the system worked, the officer asked him for identification. Gaitlan gave them his drivers license, they entered it into the computer, and moments later they arrested Gaitlan because information on the screen showed Gaitlan was wanted for a two year old armed robbery in St. Louis, Missouri.

A guy walked into a little corner store with a shotgun and demanded all the cash from the cash drawer. After the cashier put the cash in a bag, the robber saw a bottle of scotch that he wanted behind the counter on the shelf. He told the cashier to put it in the bag as well, but he refused and said "Because I don't believe you are over 21." The robber said he was, but the clerk still refused to give it to him because he didn't believe him. At this point the robber took his drivers license out of his wallet and gave it to the clerk. The clerk looked it over, and agreed that the man was in fact over 21 and he put the scotch in the bag. The robber then ran from the store with his loot. The cashier promptly called the police and gave the name and address of the robber that he got off the license. They arrested the robber two hours later.

Guns don't kill people ... (G)
Driving 40 in the fast lane kills people.
Don't shoot me, I'll move over.
Honk if you're reloading
Cover me, I'm about to change lanes.
Newest sign seen along side the road on the expressway:
   Next Exit: Gas, Food, and Ammo and: 12 gauge and over use
   TRUCK ROUTE RELOADERS use right lane

Anything You Want (G)
Michael C., 18, Sheffield Lake, Ohio, was charged with stealing his mother's credit card to pay for his 18-year-old girlfriend's breast enlargement surgery. According to a police report, Copp's mother, Gaelene Pakrandt, told officers she had closed the account because her son charged $2,100 in car repair bills.

Police said Copp reopened the account without his mother's knowledge after he found the card in a drawer. He charged $2,496 to the card to cover the surgery. Most items purchased with a stolen credit card are confiscated and returned by police. But this case is a little different.

Engineering Students (PG-13)
Two engineering students were walking across campus when one said, "Where did you get such a great bike?" The second engineer replied, "Well, I was walking along yesterday minding my own business when a beautiful woman rode up on this bike. She threw the bike to the ground, took off all her clothes and said, "Take what you want." "The second engineer nodded approvingly, "Good choice. The clothes probably wouldn't have fit."

Revelations (R)

A young female came to the ER with lower abdominal pain. During the exam and questioning the female denied being sexually active. The doctor gave her a pregnancy test anyway and it came back positive. The doctor went back to the young female's room.

Doctor: "The results of your pregnancy test came back positive. Are you sure you're not sexually active?"
Patient: "Sexually active? No, sir, I just lay there."
Doctor: "I see. Well, do you know who the father is?"
Patient: "No. Who?"

What Your Boss Really Thinks About You (G)

How to decipher employee work performance evaluations

Accepts new job assignments willingly: Never finishes a job.
Active socially: Drinks heavily.
Alert to company developments: An office gossip.
Approaches difficult problems with logic: Finds someone else to do the job.
Consults with co-workers often: Indecisive, confused, and clueless.
Consults with supervisor often: Pain in the ass.
Displays excellent intuitive judgment: Knows when to disappear.
Happy: Paid too much.
Hard worker: Usually does it the hard way.
Identifies major management problems: Complains a lot.
Indifferent to instruction: Knows more than superiors.
Internationally know: Likes to go to conferences and trade shows in Las Vegas.
Is well informed: Knows all office gossip and where all the skeletons are kept.
Inspires the cooperation of others: Gets everyone else to do the work.
Keen sense of humor: Knows lots of dirty jokes.

Keeps informed on business issues: Subscribes to Playboy and National Enquirer.
Listens well: Has no ideas of his own.
Not a desk person: Did not go to college.
Use all available resources: Takes office supplies home for personal use.
Quick thinking: Offers plausible excuses for errors.
Spends extra hours on the job: Miserable home life.
Strong adherence to principles: Stubborn.
Takes advantage of every opportunity to progress: Buys drinks for superiors.

The Architect, artist and Engineer (G)

An architect, an artist and an engineer were discussing whether it was better to spend time with the wife or a mistress.

The architect said he enjoyed time with his wife, building a solid foundation for an enduring relationship.

The artist said he enjoyed time with his mistress, because of the passion and mystery he found there.

The engineer said, "I like both."

"Both?", asked the other two.

"Yeah. If you have a wife and a mistress, they will each assume you are spending time with the other woman, and you can go to the plant and get some work done."

The Priest and the Drunk (G)

A drunk that smelled like a brewery got on a bus one day. He sat down next to a priest. The drunk's shirt was stained, his face was full of bright red lipstick and he had a half empty bottle of wine sticking out of his pocket. He opened his newspaper and started reading---a couple of minutes later he asked the priest,

"Father what causes arthritis"? "Mister, it's caused by loose living, being with cheap wicked women, too much alcohol and contempt for your fellow man".

"Well I'll be damned", the drunk muttered and returned to reading his paper.

The priest, thinking about what he said turned to the man and apologized. "I'm sorry, I didn't mean to come on so strong---how long have you had arthritis"? "I don't, father, I was just reading in the paper that the Pope has it".

Who Knows What They Would Say (R)

A baby was born that was so advanced that he could talk. He looked around the delivery room and saw the doctor. "Are you my doctor?" he asked. "Yes, I am."

The baby said "Thank you for taking such good care of me during birth." He looked at his mother and asked, "Are you my mother?" "Yes, I am," she said.

"Thank you for taking such good care of me before I was born" he said. He then looked at his father and asked "Are you my father?" "Yes, I am," his father answered. The baby motioned him close, then poked him on the forehead with his index finger 5 times, saying "I want you to know that THAT HURTS!"

The Professions (G)

The graduate with a Science degree asks, "Why does it work?"

The graduate with an Engineering degree asks, "How does it work?"

The graduate with an Accounting degree asks, "How much will it cost?"

The graduate with an Arts degree asks, "Do you want fries with that?"

Forrest Gump in Heaven (G)

The day finally arrives: Forrest Gump dies and goes to heaven. He is met at the Pearly Gates by St. Peter himself. The gates are closed, however, and Forrest approaches the gatekeeper. St. Peter says "Well Forrest, it's certainly good to see you. We have heard a lot about you. I must inform you that the place is filling up fast, and we've been administering an entrance examination for everyone. The tests are fairly short, but you need to pass before you can get into Heaven.

Forrest responds "It shore is good to be here St. Peter. I was looking forward to this. Nobody ever told me about any entrance exam. Sure hope the test ain't too hard; life was a big enough test as it was".

St. Peter goes on, "Yes, I know Forrest but the test I have for you is only three questions. Here is the first: What days of the week begin with the letter T? Second: How many seconds are there in a year? Third: What is God's first name?".

Forrest goes away to think the questions over. He returns the next day and goes up to St. Peter to try to answer the exam questions. St. Peter waves him up and says "Now that you have had a chance to think the questions over, tell me your answers." Forrest says, "Well, the first one how many days of the week begin with the letter "T?" Shucks, that ones easy. That'd be Today and Tomorrow. The Saint's eyes open wide and he exclaims "Forrest! That's not what I was thinking, but.....you do have a point though, and I guess I didn't specify, so I give you credit for that answer."

"How about the next one?" says St. Peter. "How many seconds in a year?"

"Now that one's harder" says Forrest, "but I thunk and thunk about that and I guess the only answer can be twelve."

astounded St. Peter says "Twelve! Twelve! Forrest, how in Heaven's name could you come up with twelve seconds in a year?" Forest says "Shucks, there gotta be twelve, January second, February second, March second. . . "Hold it" interrupts St. Peter. "I see where you're going with it. And I guess I see your point, though that wasn't quite what I had in mind, but I'll give you credit for that one too. Let's go on with the next and final question.

Can you tell me God's first name?" Forrest replied "Andy" when St. Peter asked how in the world he came up with the name Andy, Forrest replies, "It says so in the Bible. . "Andy walks with me, Andy talks with me."

Wife's Butt (PG-13)

A couple had been married for 15 years. One afternoon, they were working in the garden together. As the wife was bending over pulling weeds, the husband said "Hey honey, you're getting fat! Your behind is getting huge! I bet its as big as the gas grill!"

The husband, feeling he needed to prove his point, got a yardstick, measured the grill, and then measured his wife's behind. "Yep, just as I thought, just about the same size."

The wife became very angry and decided to let him do the gardening alone. She went inside, and didn't speak to him for the rest of the day.

That evening, when they went to bed, the husband cuddled up to his wife and said, "How about it, honey? How about a little hanky panky?"

The wife rolled over and turned her back to him, giving him the cold shoulder and replied, "You don't think I'm going to fire up this big gas grill for one little weenie, do you?"

Stud Rooster (PG-13)

A farmer goes out one day and buys a brand new stud rooster for his chicken coop. The young rooster walks over to the old rooster and says, "Ok, old fellow, time to retire". The old rooster says, "You can't handle all these chickens...look at what it did to me!" The young rooster replies, "Now, don't give me a hassle about this. Time for the old to step aside and the young to take over, so take a hike". The old rooster says, "Aw, c'mon....just let me have the two old hens over in the corner. I won't bother you". The young rooster says, "Scram! Beat it! You're washed up! I'm taking over!" So the old rooster thinks for a minute and then says to the young rooster, "I'll tell you what, young fellow, I'll have a race with you around the farmhouse. Whoever wins the race gets domain of the chicken coop". The young rooster says, "You know I'm going to beat you, old man, so just to be fair, I'm even going to give you a head start". They line up in back of the farmhouse, get a chicken to cluck "Go!" and the old rooster takes off running. About 15 seconds later, the young rooster takes off after him. They round the front of the farmhouse and the young rooster is only about 5 inches behind the old rooster and gaining fast.
The farmer, sitting on the porch, looks up, sees what's going on, grabs his shotgun and BOOM!, he blows the young rooster to bits. He sadly shakes his head and says, "Dammit, third gay rooster I bought this week!"

Good news, Bad news (G)

An artist asked the gallery owner if there had been any interest in his paintings on display at that time.

"I have good news and bad news," the owner replied. "The good news is that a gentleman inquired about your work and wondered if it would appreciate in value after your death."

"When I told him it would, he bought all 15 of your paintings."

"That's wonderful," the artist exclaimed.
"What's the bad news?"
"The guy was your doctor..."

A Trip To The Zoo (G)

It's a beautiful warm day and a man and his wife are at the Zoo. She's wearing a cute loose-fitting, pink spring dress, sleeveless with straps. As they walk through the ape exhibit and pass in front of a very large gorilla, the beast goes crazy. He jumps up on the bars, holding on with one hand and his feet, grunting and pounding his chest with his free hand. The gorilla is obviously excited at the pretty lady in the wavy dress. The husband, noticing the excitement, proposes that his wife tease the poor fellow. The husband suggests she pucker her lips, wiggle her bottom, and play along. She does, and the gorilla gets even more excited, making noises that would wake the dead. Then the husband suggests that she let one of her straps fall. She does, and the gorilla is just about to tear the bars down. "Now try lifting your dress up your thighs." This drives the gorilla absolutely crazy.

Suddenly, the husband grabs his wife by the arm, rips open the cage door, slings her in with the gorilla and slams the door shut.

"Now, tell HIM you have a headache!"

The Mental Patient (G)

After hearing that one of the patients in a mental hospital had saved another from a suicide attempt by pulling him out of a bathtub, the director reviewed the rescuer's file and called him into his office.

"Mr. James, your records and your heroic behavior indicate

that you're ready to go home. I'm only sorry that the man you saved later succeeded in killing himself with a rope around the neck."

"Oh, he didn't kill himself," Mr. James replied. "I hung him up to dry."

A Pant Problem (PG-13)

The Little Johnny was 8 years old when his parents decided to have him circumcised (looking different than dad, other kids, etc.). After a few days of recovery, the boy went back to school. After about an hour, the pain was really starting to bother him so he asked if he could see the school nurse. He went to see her, but was too embarrassed to tell her what the problem was. She suggested that he call his Mom and see if she could come and get him. The nurse waited in the other room while the call was made. After a few minutes the little boy came out and started walking back to class, but the nurse noticed that his penis was hanging out of his pants. She said, "Johnny, what are you doing? You can't walk around like that." He replied, "Well I told my Mom how much I hurt and she said that if I could just stick it out till lunchtime she would come pick me up then."

An optimist vs. a pessimist: (G)

An avid duck hunter was in the market for a new bird dog. His search ended when he found a dog that could actually walk on water to retrieve a duck. Shocked by his find, he was sure none of his friends would ever believe him.

He decided to try to break the news to a friend of his, a pessimist by nature, and invited him to hunt with him and his new dog. As they waited by the shore, a flock of ducks flew by.

They fired, and a duck fell. The dog responded and jumped into the water. The dog, however, did not sink but instead walked across the water to retrieve the bird, never getting more than his paws wet.

The friend saw everything but did not say a single word. On the drive home the hunter asked his friend, "Did you notice anything unusual about my new dog?"

"I sure did," responded his friend. "He can't swim."

Darwin Award Winner (G)

(The late) John Pernicky and his friend, (the late) Sal Hawkins, of the great state of Washington, who decided to attend a local Metallica concert at the Amphitheater at Gorge, Washington. Having no tickets (but 18 beers among them) they thought it would be easy enough to hop over the nine-foot high fence and sneak into the show. The two friend-spulled their pickup truck over to the fence and the plan was for John--100 pounds heavier than Sal - to hop over, and then assist his friend over the fence. Unfortunately for John, there was a 30 foot drop on the other side of the fence. Having heaved himself over, he found himself crashing through a tree.

His fall was abruptly halted by a large branch which snagged him by his shorts. Dangling from the tree, with one arm broken, John looked down and saw a group of bushes below him. Possibly figuring the bushes would break his fall, John removed his pocket knife and proceeded to cut away his shorts to free himself from the tree. Finally free, John crashed below into Holly bushes.

The sharp leaves scratched his entire body and now being without his shorts, he was the unwilling victim of a holly branch penetrating his rectal cavity. To make matters worse, his pocket knife proceeded to fall with him and landed three inches into his left thigh. Seeing his friend in considerable pain and agony, Sal decided to throw him a rope and pull him to safety by tying the rope to the pickup truck and slowly driving away. However, in his drunken state, Sal put the truck into reverse rather than first, and crashed through the fence, landing on and killing his friend. Sal was thrown from the truck, suffered massive internal injuries and died at the scene.

Police arrived to find a pickup truck with its driver thrown 100 feet from the truck. Upon moving the truck, they found John under it, half naked, with scratches, a holly stick up his rectum, a knife in his thigh, and his shorts dangling from the tree branches 25 feet in the air.

HOW TO SCREW UP AN INTERVIEW

We surveyed top personnel executives of 100 major American corporations and asked for stories of unusual behavior by job applicants.
1. "...stretched out on the floor to fill out the job application."
2. "She wore a Walkman and said she could listen to me and the music at the same time."
3. "A balding candidate abruptly excused himself. Returned to office a few minutes later, wearing a hairpiece."
4. "... asked to see interviewer's resume to see if the personnel executive was qualified to judge the candidate."
5. "... announced she hadn't had lunch and proceeded to eat a hamburger and French fries in the interviewer's office - wiping the ketchup on her sleeve"
6. "Stated that, if he were hired, he would demonstrate his loyalty by having the corporate logo tattooed on his forearm."
7. "Interrupted to phone his therapist for advice on answering specific interview questions."
8. "When I asked him about his hobbies, he stood up and started tap dancing around my office."
9. "At the end of the interview, while I stood there dumbstruck, he went through my purse, took out a brush, brushed his hair, and left."
10. ".. pulled out a Polaroid camera and snapped a flash pic-

ture of me. Said he collected photos of everyone who interviewed him."

11. "Said he wasn't interested because the position paid too much."
12. "While I was on a long-distance phone call, the applicant took out a copy of Penthouse, and looked through the photos only, stopping longest at the centerfold."
13. "During the interview, an alarm clock went off from the candidate's brief case. He took it out, shut it off, apologized and said he had to leave for another interview."
14. "A telephone call came in for the job applicant. It was from his wife. His side of the conversation went like this: "Which company? When do I start? What's the salary?" I said, "I assume you're not interested in conducting the interview any further." He promptly responded, "I am as long as you'll pay me more. "I didn't hire him, but later found out there was no other job offer. It was a scam to get a higher offer."
15. "His attaché [case] opened when he picked it up and the contents spilled, revealing ladies' undergarments and assorted makeup and perfume."
16. "Candidate said he really didn't want to get a job, but the unemployment office needed proof that he was looking for one."
17. "... asked who the lovely babe was, pointing to the picture on my desk. When I said it was my wife, he asked if she was home now and wanted my phone number. I called security,"
18. "Pointing to a black case he carried into my office, he said that if he was not hired, the bomb would go off. Disbelieving, I began to state why he would never be hired and that I was going to call the police. He then reached down to the case, flipped a switch and ran. No one was injured, but I did need to get a new desk."

Last Request (G)

An elderly man was at home, dying in bed. He smelled the aroma of his favorite chocolate chip cookies baking. He wanted one last cookie before he died.

He fell out of bed, crawled to the landing, rolled down the stairs, and crawled into the kitchen where his wife was busily baking cookies. With waning strength he crawled to the table and was just barely able to lift his withered arm to the cookie sheet.

As he grasped a warm, moist, chocolate chip cookie, his favorite kind, his wife suddenly whacked his hand with a spatula. "Why?" he whispered. "Why did you do that?"

"They're for the funeral."

Real court transcriptions, word for word. (G)

Q: What gear were you in at the moment of the impact?
A: Gucci sweats and Reeboks.

Q: What was the first thing your husband said to you when he woke that morning?
A: He said, "Where am I, Cathy?"
Q: And why did that upset you?
A: My name is Susan.

Q: Sir, what is your IQ?
A: Well, I can see pretty well, I think.

Q: Did you blow your horn or anything?
A: After the accident?
Q: Before the accident.
A: Sure, I played for ten years. I even went to school for it.

Q: Do you know if your daughter has ever been involved in the voodoo or occult?
A: We both do.

Q: Voodoo?
A: We do.
Q: You do?
A: Yes, voodoo.

Q: Trooper, when you stopped the defendant, were your red and blue lights flashing?
A: Yes.
Q: Did the defendant say anything when she got out of her car?
A: Yes, sir.
Q: What did she say?
A: What disco am I at?

Lazyitis (G)

The man told his doctor that he wasn't able to do all the things around the house that he used to do. When the examination was complete, he said, "Now, Doc, I can take it. Tell me in plain English what is wrong with me."

"Well, in plain English," the doctor replied, "you're just lazy."

"Okay," said the man. "Now give me the medical term so I can tell my wife."

Big Decision (PG-13)

A man had been dating three women for a while and finally decided it was time to settle down. However, he didn't know which of the three to marry. He devised a little test and based on how the three responded, he hoped to be able to make his selection.

He gave each of them $10,000 and told them to spend it however they wanted. The first woman bought herself a fur coat, six new outfits and took a vacation to the Bahamas. The second woman spent it all on him... a new set of golf clubs,

scuba diving equipment and sent him to the Bahamas. The third woman invested it all, tripled her money in three weeks, and paid for a five week cruise for both she and the man.
So which woman did he marry???

The one with the big breasts!

"Bathing Like A Man" (G)
Take off clothes while sitting on the edge of the bed and leave them in a pile on the floor.
Walk to bathroom wearing a towel. If you see your girl friend/wife along the way, flash her.
Look at your manly physique in the mirror and suck in your gut to see if you have pecs. (no)
Turn on the water.
Check for pecs again. (still no)
Get in the shower.
Don't bother to look for a washcloth. (You don't use one).
Wash your face.
Wash your armpits.
Wash your privates and surrounding area.
Wash your butt.
Shampoo your hair. (Do not use conditioner)
Make a shampoo Mohawk.
Draw a smilie face on fogged up shower door.
Open the door and look at yourself in the mirror.
Pee.
Rinse off and get out of the shower.
Return to the bedroom wearing a towel. If you pass your girlfriend/wife, flash her.

First Trick (R)

The new hooker had just finished her first trick. When she came back down the street, the seasoned veterans all gathered around to hear all the details.

She said, "Well, he was a big, muscular and handsome marine."

"Well, what did he want you to do?" they all ask.

She said. "I told him that a straight lay was $100, but he said he didn't have that much.

So I told him a blow job would be $75, but he didn't have that much either. Finally I said, "Well, how much do you have?"

"The marine said he only had $25."

So, I told him. "For $25 all I can give you is a hand job." He agreed, and after getting the finances straight, he pulled it out. I put one hand on it. Then, I put the other hand above that one." She paused, raised her eyebrows, and then continued, "Then I put the first hand above the second hand..."

"Oh my God!" they all exclaimed, "it must have been huge! Then what did you do?"

"I loaned him $75!"

Nude Beach (PG-13)

Two parents take their son on a vacation and go to a nude beach. The father goes for a walk on the beach and the son goes and plays in the water. The son comes running up to his mom and says,

"Mommy, I saw ladies with boobies a lot bigger than yours!"

The mom says, "The bigger they are, the dumber they are."

So he goes back to play. Minutes later he runs back and says, "Mommy, I saw men with dingers a lot bigger than Daddy's!"

The mom says, "The bigger they are, the dumber they are."

So he goes back to play. Several minutes later he comes running back and says, "Mommy, I just saw Daddy talking to the dumbest lady I ever saw and the more and more he talked, the dumber and dumber he got!"

Snappy Comeback (PG-13)
An older gent had an appointment to see a urologist who shared an office with several other doctors. The waiting room was filled with patients.

He approached the receptionist desk. The receptionist was a large imposing woman who looked like a wrestler. He gave her his name. In a VERY LOUD VOICE the receptionist said, "YES, I HAVE YOUR NAME HERE; YOU WANT TO SEE THE DOCTOR ABOUT IMPOTENCE, RIGHT?"

All of the patients in the waiting room snapped their head around to look at the very embarrassed man.

He recovered quickly though, and in an equally loud voice replied, "NO, I'VE COME TO INQUIRE ABOUT A SEX CHANGE OPERATION; AND I'D LIKE THE SAME DOCTOR THAT DID YOURS."

Only in America!?! (G)
Only in America.....can a pizza get to your house faster than an ambulance...

Only in America.....are there handicap parking places in front of a skating rink..

Only in America.....do drugstores make the sick walk all the way to the back of the store to get their prescriptions...

Only in America.....do people order double cheese burgers, a large fry, and a diet coke...

Only in America.....do we leave cars worth thousands of dollars in the driveway and leave useless junk in the garage...

Only in America.....do we use answering machines to screen

calls and then have call waiting so we won't miss a call from someone we didn't want to talk to in the first place...

THE PERFECT DAY - FOR HIM (R)
6:00 Alarm
6:15 Blow job
6:30 Massive satisfying dump while reading the sports section
7:00 Breakfast: rump steak and eggs, coffee and toast, all cooked by naked buxom wench
7:30 Limo arrives
7:45 Several Whiskeys en-route to airport
9:15 Flight in personal Lear Jet
9:30 Limo to Riverside Oaks Golf Club (blow job en-route)
9:45 Play front nine (2 under)
11:45 Satisfying Lunch, 3 lagers and a bottle of Dom Perignon
12:15 Blow job
12:30 Play back nine (4 under)
2:15 Limo back to the airport (Several Whiskeys)
2:30 Fly to Monte Carlo
3:30 Late afternoon fishing excursion with all female crew (all nude)
4:30 Land world record Marlin (978 lb.) - on light tackle
5:00 Fly home, massage and hand job by naked Elle McPherson
6:45 F*ck, Shower and Shave
7:00 Watch news: marijuana and porn legalized, great sports highlights
7:30 Dinner: lobster appetizers, Dom Perignon (1953), big juicy fillet steak followed by Ice-cream served on a pair of tits
9:00 Napoleon Brandy and Cohuna cigar in front of wall size TV as you watch superbowl with male friends

9:30 Sex with three women (all with lesbian tendencies)
11:00 Massage and Jacuzzi with tasty pizza snacks and a cleansing ale
11:30 A night cap blowjob
11:45 In bed alone
11:50 A 12 second fart which changes note 4 times and forces the dog to leave the room

---

Parrot joke (PG-13)

A woman was thinking about finding a pet to help keep her company at home. She decided she would like to find a beautiful parrot; it wouldn't be as much work as, say, a dog, and it would be fun to hear it speak.

She went to a pet shop and immediately spotted a large beautiful parrot. She went to the owner of the store and asked how much. The owner said $50.00.

Delighted that such a rare looking and beautiful bird wasn't more expensive, she agreed to buy it. The owner looked at her and said, "Look, I should tell you first that this bird used to live in a whorehouse. Sometimes it says pretty vulgar stuff.

The woman thought about this, but decided she had to have the bird. She said she would buy it anyway. The pet shop owner sold her the bird and she took it home. She hung the bird's cage up in her living room and waited for it to say something. The bird looked around the room, then at her, and said, "New house, new madam."

The woman was a bit shocked at the implication, but then thought that's not so bad. A couple of hours later, the woman's two daughters returned from school. When they inspected the bird, it looked at them and said, "New house, new madam, new whores..."

The girls and the woman were a bit offended at first, but then began to laugh about the situation. A couple of hours later, the woman's husband came home from work. The bird looked at him and said, "New house, new madam, new whores....Hi Phil!!"

Good Deeds (G)

His name was Fleming, and he was a poor Scottish farmer. One day while trying to eke out a living for his family, he heard a cry for help coming from a nearby bog.

He dropped his tools and ran to the bog. There, mired to his waist in black muck, was a terrified boy, screaming and struggling to free himself. Farmer Fleming saved the lad from what could have been a slow and terrifying death.

The next day, a fancy carriage pulled up to the Scotsman's sparse surroundings. An elegantly dressed nobleman stepped out an introduced himself as the father of the boy Farmer Fleming had saved.

"I want to repay you," said the nobleman. "You saved my son's life."

"No, I can't accept payment for what I did," the Scottish farmer replied, waving off the offer. At that moment, the farmer's own son came to the door of the family hovel.

"Is that your son?" the nobleman asked.

"Yes," the farmer replied proudly.

"I'll make you a deal. Let me take him and give him a good education. If the lad is anything like his father, he'll grow to a man you can be proud of."

And that he did. In time, Farmer Fleming's son graduated from St. Mary's Hospital Medical School in London, and went on to become known throughout the world as the noted Sir Alexander Fleming, the discoverer of Penicillin.

Years afterward, the nobleman's son was stricken with pneumonia.

What saved him? Penicillin.

The name of the nobleman? Lord Randolph Churchill. His son's name? Sir Winston Churchill. Someone once said what goes around comes around.

Letters Of Recommendations For Employees (G)

Have to write a letter of recommendation for that fired employee? Here are a few suggested phrases:

For the chronically absent:
"A man like him is hard to find."
"It seemed her career was just taking off."

For the office drunk:
"I feel his real talent is wasted here."
"We generally found him loaded with work to do."
"Every hour with him was a happy hour."

For an employee with no ambition:
"You would indeed be fortunate to get this person to work for you."
"He could not care less about the number of hours he had to put in."

For an employee who is so unproductive that the job is better left unfilled:
"I can assure you that no person would be better for the job."

The Pope (PG-13)

A shy gentleman was preparing to board a plane when he heard that the Pope was on the same flight. "This is exciting," thought the gentleman. "I've always been a big fan of the Pope. Perhaps I'll be able to see him in person." Imagine his surprise when the Pope sat down in the seat next to him for the flight. Still, the gentleman was too shy to speak to the Pontiff. Shortly after takeoff, the Pope began a crossword puzzle. "This is fantastic," thought the gentleman. "I'm really good at crosswords. Perhaps, if the Pope gets stuck, he'll ask me for assistance." Almost immediately, the Pope turned to the gentleman and said,

"Excuse me, but do you know a four letter word referring to a woman that ends in 'u-n-t'?" Only one word leapt to mind... "My goodness," thought the gentleman, "I can't tell the Pope that. There must be another." The gentleman thought for quite a while, then it hit him. Turning to the pope, the gentleman said, "I think you're looking for the word 'aunt'."

"Of course," said the Pope. "Do you have an eraser?"

Search For Perfection (G)

A friend asked a gentleman how it is that he never married? Replied the gentleman, "Well, I guess I just never met the right woman ... I guess I've been looking for the perfect girl."

"Oh, come on now," said the friend, "Surely you have met at least one girl that you wanted to marry."

"Yes, there was a girl... once. I guess she was the one perfect girl; the only perfect girl I really ever met. She was just the right everything... I really mean that she was the perfect girl for me."

"Well, why didn't you marry her," asked the friend.

"She was looking for the perfect man."

Work vs. Prison (G)

IN PRISON you spend the majority of your time in an 8x10 cell.
   AT WORK you spend most of your time in a 6x8 cubicle.
IN PRISON you get time off for good behavior.
   AT WORK you get rewarded for good behavior with more work.
IN PRISON they allow your family and friends to visit.
   AT WORK you cannot even speak to your family and friends.
IN PRISON all expenses are paid by taxpayers with no work required.

AT WORK you get to pay all the expenses to go to work and then they deduct taxes from your salary to pay for prisoners.
IN PRISON there are wardens who are often sadistic.
AT WORK they are called managers.

Real Friends (G)
A simple friend can stand by you when you are right, but a
A real friend will stand by you even when you are wrong.
A simple friend identifies himself when he calls.
A real friend doesn't have to.
A simple friend opens a conversation with a full news bulletin on his life.
A real friend says, "What's new with you?"
A simple friend thinks the problems you whine about are recent.
A real friend says, "You've been whining about the same thing for 14 years. Get off your duff and do something about it."
A real friend comes early to help you cook and stays late to help you clean.
A simple friend hates it when you call after he has gone to bed.
A simple friend wonders about your romantic history.
A real friend could blackmail you with it.
A simple friend, when visiting, acts like a guest.
A real friend opens your refrigerator and helps himself/herself.
A simple friend thinks the friendship is over when you have an argument.
A real friend knows that it's not a friendship until after you've had a fight.

Redneck Driving Etiquette (G)

Do not lay rubber while traveling in a funeral procession.
Dim your headlights for approaching vehicles, even if the gun is loaded and the deer is in sight.
When approaching a four-way stop, the vehicle with the largest tires always has the right of way.
When sending your wife down the road with a gas can, it is impolite to ask her to bring back beer.
Do not remove the seats from the car so that all your kids can fit in.

New Bike (PG-13)

A father came home from a long business trip to find his son riding a very fancy new 10 speed bike. "Where did you get the money for the bike? It must have cost $300."

"Easy, Dad," the boy replied. "I earned it hiking." "Come on," the father said. "Tell me the truth." "That is the truth," the boy replied.

"Every night you were gone, Mr. Reynolds from the grocery store would come over to see Mom. He'd give me a $20 bill and tell me to take a hike!"

Top 10 Rejection Lines Given By Women (and what they actually mean)

10. I think of you as a brother. (You remind me of that inbred banjo-playing geek in "Deliverance.")
9. There's a slight difference in our ages. (I don't want to do my dad.)
8. I'm not attracted to you in 'that' way. (You are the ugliest dork I've ever laid eyes on.)

7. My life is too complicated right now. (I don't want you spending the whole night or else you may hear phone calls from all the other guys I'm seeing.)
6. I've got a boyfriend. (I prefer my male cat and a half gallon of Ben and Jerry's.)
5. I don't date men where I work. (I wouldn't date you if you were in the same 'solar system', much less the same building.)
4. It's not you, it's me. (It's you.)
3. I'm concentrating on my career. (Even something as boring and unfulfilling as my job is better than dating you.)
2. I'm celibate. (I've sworn off only the men like you.)
1. Let's be friends. (I want you to stay around so I can tell you in excruciating detail about all the other men I meet and have sex with. It's the male perspective thing.)

It Takes a Rocket Scientist (G)

Scientists at NASA have developed a gun built specifically to launch dead chickens at the windshields of airliners, military jets and the space shuttle, all traveling at maximum velocity. The idea is to simulate the frequent incidents of collisions with airborne fowl to test the strength of the windshields. British engineers heard about the gun and were eager to test it on the windshields of their new high speed trains. Arrangements were made. When the gun was fired, the engineers stood shocked as the chicken hurtled out of the barrel, crashed into the shatterproof shield, smashed it to smithereens, crashed through the control console, snapped the engineer's backrest in two and embedded itself in the back wall of the cabin. Horrified Britons sent NASA the disastrous results of the experiment, along with the designs of the windshield, and begged the U.S. scientists for suggestions. NASA's response was just one sentence.
"Thaw the chicken."

How Kids Learn (R)
Little Gregory wakes up in the middle of the night feeling alone and scared. He goes into his mother's room for comfort and he sees his mom standing naked in front of the mirror. She is rubbing her chest and groaning, "I want a man, I want a man." Shaking his head in bewilderment, Gregory takes off to bed. Next night the same thing happens. On the third night, Gregory wakes up and goes into his mom's room but this time there is a man in bed with his mom. Gregory hoofs back to his room and whips off his pajamas, rubs his chest and groans "I want a bike, I want a bike."

"SIGNS" of the Nineties (PG-13)
Friends don't let friends take home ugly men.
   * Women's restroom, Dewey Beach, DE

The best way to a man's heart is to saw his breast plate open.
   * Women's restroom, Murphy's, Champaign, IL

If life is a waste of time, and time is a waste of life, then let's all get wasted together and have the time of our lives.
   * Armand's Pizza. Washington, DC

God made pot. Man made beer. Who do you trust?
   * The Irish Times. Washington, DC

No matter how good she looks, some other guy is sick and tired of putting up with her sh*t.
   *Men's Room, Linda's Bar and Grill. Chapel Hill, North Carolina.

To do is to be. -Descartes
   To be is to do. -Voltaire
   Do be do be do. -Frank Sinatra
   * Men's restroom, Greasewood Flats. Scottsdale, Arizona.

At the feast of ego, everyone leaves hungry.
   * Bentley's House of Coffee and Tea, Tucson, Arizona.

It's hard to make a comeback when you haven't been any where.
   * Written in the dust on the back of a bus, Wickenburg, Arizona.

Express Lane: Five beers or less.

* Sign over one of the urinals, Ed Debevic's, Phoenix, AZ. No wonder you always go home alone.
   * Sign over mirror in Men's restroom, Ed Debevic's, Beverly Hills,CA

Under the Restaurant Table (PG-13)

John and Mary were having dinner in a very fine restaurant. Their waitress, taking another order at a table a few paces away, noticed that John was ever so slowly, silently sliding down his chair and under the table, while Mary acted quite unconcerned.

Their waitress watched as John slid all the way down his chair and out of sight under the table. Still, Mary appeared calm and unruffled, apparently unaware that dear John had disappeared under the table.

After the waitress finished taking the order, she came over to the table and said to the woman, "Pardon me, ma'am, but I think your husband just slid under the table."

The woman calmly looked up at her and replied firmly, "Oh, no he didn't. In fact, he just walked in the front door."

How Did I Do (PG-13)

A guy met a girl at a nightclub, and she invited him back to her place for the night. When they arrived at her house, they went right into her bedroom. The guy saw that the room was filled with stuffed animals. There were hundreds of them all over the place. Giant stuffed animals were on top of the wardrobe. Large stuffed animals were on the bookshelf and on the window sill, and a lot of smaller stuffed animals were on the bottom shelf. Much later, after they had sex, he turned to her and asked, "So...how was I?"

"Well," she said, "you can take anything from the bottom shelf."

Murder or Suicide? (PG-13)

At the 1994 annual awards dinner given for Forensic Science, AAFS president Dr. Don Harper Mills astounded his audience with the legal complications of a bizarre death:

On March 23, 1994, the medical examiner viewed the body of Ronald Opus and concluded that he died from a shotgun wound to the head. Mr. Opus had jumped from the top of a ten story building intending to commit suicide.

He left a note to that effect indicating his despondency. As he fell past the ninth floor his life was interrupted by a shotgun blast passing through a window which killed him instantly. Neither the shooter nor the dead man was aware that a safety net had been installed just below at the eighth floor level to protect some building workers and that Ronald Opus would not have been able to complete his suicide the way he planned. "Ordinarily," Dr. Mills continued, "a person who sets out to commit suicide and ultimately succeeds even though the mechanism might not be what he intended" is still defined as committing suicide. That Mr. Opus was shot during what would apparently have been an unsuccessful suicide attempt because of the safety net, caused the medical examiner to feel that he had a homicide on his hands.

The room on the ninth floor where the shotgun blast emanated was occupied by an elderly man and his wife. They were arguing vigorously, and he was threatening her with a shotgun. The man was so upset when he pulled the trigger that he completely missed his wife and the pellets went through the window striking Mr. Opus as he passed by outside. When someone, intending to kill person "A," kills person "B" instead; someone is still guilty of murder. When confronted with a murder charge the old man and his wife were both adamant; they both said they thought the shotgun was unloaded. The old man said it was his long standing habit to threaten his wife with the unloaded shotgun. He had no intention to murder her. Therefore, the Killing of Mr. Opus appeared to be an accident; that is, the gun had been accidentally loaded. The continuing investigation turned up a witness who saw the old couple's son loading the shotgun about six weeks prior to the fatal accident. It transpired that the old lady had cut off her son's financial support and the son, knowing the propensity of his father to use the shotgun threateningly, loaded the gun with the expectation that his father would shoot his mother. The case now reverts back to one of murder on the part of the son. Now comes The final twist! Further investigation revealed that the couple's son was In fact, Ronald Opus. He had become increasingly despondent over his failed attempt to engineer his mother's murder. This led him to jump off the ten story building on March 23rd, only to be killed by the shotgun blast passing through the ninth floor window. The son had actually murdered himself so the medical examiner closed the case and declared it a suicide.

Shocking News (PG-13)

A very elderly couple is having an elegant dinner to celebrate their 75th wedding anniversary. The old man leans forward and says softly to his wife, "Dear, there is something that I must ask you. It has always bothered me that our tenth child never quite looked like the rest of our children. Now I want to assure you that these 75 years have been the most wonderful experience I could have ever hoped for, and your answer cannot take all that away. But, I must know, did he have a different father?"

The wife drops her head, unable to look her husband in the eye, she paused for a moment and then confessed. "Yes. Yes he did."

The old man is very shaken, the reality of what his wife was admitting hit him harder than he had expected. With a tear in his eye he asks "Who? Who was he? Who was the father?"

Again the old woman drops her head, saying nothing at first as she tried to muster the courage to tell the truth to her husband. Then, finally, she says, "You."

Four Guys in a Car (G)

Four guys are driving cross-country together-- 1 from Idaho, 1 from Iowa, 1 from Florida, and the last 1 is from New York. On down the road, the man from Idaho pulls potatoes from his bag and throws them out the window. The Iowa man turns to him and asks, "What the hell are you doing?" The man from Idaho says, "Man, we have so many of these things in Idaho, they're laying around on the ground. I'm sick of looking at them!" A few miles down the road, the man from Iowa pulls husks of corn from his bag and throws them out the window. The man from Florida asks "What are you doing?" The man from Iowa replies, "Man, we have so many of these damned things in Iowa I'm sick of them!" Inspired by the others, the man from Florida opens the car door and pushes the New Yorker out.

Sherlock Holmes (G)

Sherlock Holmes and Dr. Watson went on a camping trip. After a good meal and a bottle of wine they lay down for the night, and went to sleep.

Some hours later, Holmes awoke and nudged his faithful friend. "Watson, look up at the sky and tell me what you see."

Watson replied, "I see millions and millions of stars."

"What does that tell you?"

Watson pondered for a minute. "Astronomically, it tells me that there are millions of galaxies and potentially billions of planets. Horologically, I deduce that the time is approximately a quarter past three. Theologically, I can see that God is all powerful and that we are small and insignificant. Meteorologically, I suspect that we will have a beautiful day tomorrow. What does it tell you?"

Sherlock Holmes was silent for a minute, then spoke. "Watson, you ########. Some ####### has stolen our tent."

Mischievous Boys (G)

A couple had two little boys, ages 8 and 10, who were excessively mischievous. The two were always getting into trouble and their parents could be assured that if any mischief occurred in their town their two young sons were in some way involved. The parents were at their wits end as to what to do about their sons' behavior.

The mother had heard that a clergyman in town had been successful in disciplining children in the past, so she asked her husband if he thought they should send the boys to speak with the clergyman. The husband said, "We might as well. We need to do something before I really lose my temper!" The clergyman agreed to speak with the boys, but asked to see them individually.

The 8 year old went to meet with him first. The clergyman sat the boy down and asked him sternly, "Where is God?" The boy made no response, so the clergyman repeated the question in an even sterner tone, "Where is God?" Again the boy made no attempt to answer. So the clergyman raised his voice even more and shook his finger in the boy's face, "WHERE IS GOD?"

At that the boy bolted from the room and ran directly home, slamming himself in the closet. His older brother followed him into the closet and said, "What happened?"

The younger brother replied, "We are in BIG trouble this time. God is missing and they think we did it."

Too Tricky (PG-13)

There was an old professor who started every class with a vulgar joke. After one particularly nasty example, the women in the class decided to walk out the next time he started.

The professor got wind of this plot, so the next morning he walked in and said: "Good morning, class. Did you hear the one about the shortage of whores in India?"

With that, all the women stood up and headed for the door. "Wait, ladies," cried the professor. "The boat doesn't leave until tomorrow!"

Best Friends (G)

Jack decided to go skiing with his buddy, Bob. They loaded up Jack's minivan and headed north. After driving for a few hours, they got caught in a terrible blizzard. They pulled into a nearby farm house and asked the attractive lady who answered the door if they could spend the night.

"I realize it's terrible weather out there and I have this huge house all to myself, but I'm recently widowed," she explained, "and I'm afraid the neighbors will talk if I let you stay in my house."

"Not to worry," Jack said, we'll be happy to sleep in the barn, and if the weather breaks, we'll be gone at first light. The lady agreed and the two men found their way to the barn and settled in for the night. Come morning, the weather had cleared and they got on their way and enjoyed a great weekend of skiing.

About nine months later, Jack got an unexpected letter from an attorney. It took him a few minutes to figure it out, but he finally determined that it was from the attorney of that attractive widow he met on the ski weekend.

He dropped in on his friend Bob and asked: "Bob, do you remember that good-looking widow from the farm we stayed at on our ski holiday up North."

"Yes, I do."

"Did you happen to get up in the middle of the night, go up to the house and have sex with her?"

"Yes," he said, a little embarrassed about being found out, "I have to admit that I did."

"And did you happen to use my name instead of telling her your name?"

Bob's face turned red and he said, "Yeah, sorry buddy, I'm afraid I did. Why do you ask?"

"No need to apologize, Bob. She just died and left me everything!

Element Name: MAN
Symbol: XY
Atomic Weight: (180+/-50)

Physical properties: Solid at room temperature, but gets bent out of shape easily. Fairly dense and sometimes flaky. Difficult to find a pure sample. Due to rust, aging samples are unable to conduct electricity as easily as young samples.
Chemical properties: Attempts to bond with WO any chance it can get. Also tends to form strong bonds with itself.
Becomes explosive when mixed with KD (Element: Child) for prolonged period of time. Neutralize by saturating with alcohol.
Usage: None known. Possibly good methane source. Good specimens are able to produce large quantities on command.
Caution: In the absence of WO, this element rapidly decomposes and begins to smell.

Element Name: WOMAN
Symbol: WO
Atomic Weight: (don't even go there)

Physical properties: Generally round in form. Boils at nothing and may freeze at any time. Melts whenever treated properly. Very bitter if mishandled.

Chemical properties: Very active. Highly unstable. Possesses strong affinity with gold, silver, platinum, and precious stones. Volatile when left alone. Able to absorb great amounts of exotic food. Turns slightly green when placed next to a shinier specimen.

Usage: Highly ornamental. An extremely good catalyst for dispersion of wealth. Probably the most powerful income reducing agent known.

Caution: Highly explosive in inexperienced hands.

ORDER FORM

Telephone Orders
Word Association Publishers
Call Toll Free: 1(800) 827-7903
Have your AMEX, VISA or MASTERCard ready.

On-line Orders
Orders@wordassociation.com

McFool's© Internet Humor
Price $10.95

Quantity ordered_____ **Total price**_____

Name: _____

Address: _____

City: _____ State: _____ Zip: _____

Telephone: (_____) _____

Please add sales tax to books shipped to Hawaii address.

Shipping:
$4.00 for the first book and $2.00 for each additional book.

Payment:
☐ Cheque
☐ Credit card: ☐ VISA,   ☐ MasterCard

Card number:_____

Name on Card:_____ Exp. date:_____ / _____

Call toll free and order now

ORDER FORM

Telephone Orders
Word Association Publishers
Call Toll Free: 1(800) 827-7903
Have your AMEX, VISA or MASTERCard ready.

On-line Orders
Orders@wordassociation.com

McFool's© Internet Humor
Price $10.95

Quantity ordered_____ **Total price**_____

Name: _____

Address: _____

City: _____ State: _____ Zip: _____

Telephone: (_____) _____

Please add sales tax to books shipped to Hawaii address.

Shipping:
$4.00 for the first book and $2.00 for each additional book.

Payment:
☐ Cheque
☐ Credit card: ☐ VISA,   ☐ MasterCard

Card number:_____

Name on Card:_____ Exp. date:_____ / _____

Call toll free and order now

ORDER FORM

Telephone Orders
Word Association Publishers
Call Toll Free: 1(800) 827-7903
Have your AMEX, VISA or MASTERCard ready.

On-line Orders
Orders@wordassociation.com

McFool's© Internet Humor
Price $10.95

Quantity ordered_____ **Total price**_____

Name: _____

Address: _____

City: _____ State: _____ Zip: _____

Telephone: (_____) _____

Please add sales tax to books shipped to Hawaii address.

Shipping:
$4.00 for the first book and $2.00 for each additional book.

Payment:
☐ Cheque
☐ Credit card: ☐ VISA,   ☐ MasterCard

Card number:_____

Name on Card:_____ Exp. date:_____ / _____

Call toll free and order now